W9-ASJ-670

TALES

told by

Hazrat Inayat Khan

Volumes now available in the series

THE COLLECTED WORKS OF HAZRAT INAYAT KHAN

Tales
Nature Meditations
The Unity of Religious Ideals
Mastery Through Accomplishment
The Soul Whence and Whither
The Complete Sayings of Hazrat Inayat Khan

'TALES'

told by
Hazrat Inayat Khan

Sufi Order Publications
New Lebanon, New York
1980

Tales Told by Hazrat Inayat Khan

SUFI ORDER PUBLICATIONS
P.O. Box 568
Lebanon Springs, N.Y. 12114

Library of Congress Catalog Card Number 80-52548

Printed in the United States of America

ISBN 0-930872-15-0

EDITOR'S NOTE

In this volume we have gathered together many of the stories told by Hazrat Inayat Khan to his disciples in the West. A collection of the stories was culled by Sheikh Mansur Johnson from Hazrat Inayat Khan's published works and privately printed in 1975. Using that compilation as a foundation, we have added many stories from his unpublished writings as well.

For the most part, explanations and commentaries have been omitted from this edition. Hazrat Inayat Khan's sometimes extensive comments can be found in the previously published material.

MUNIR GRAHAM

HAZRAT INAYAT KHAN

May I speak something very personal and deep about the author?

When I was living in Mexico in 1964, I had a vision, among many, about some teachings. Not a teacher, some teachings.

When I finally found these teachings, I was so happy. I felt home. They were so simple. Nothing complex or puzzling. Just very clear. Like my soul.

I found them in the books called *The Sufi Message of Hazrat Inayat Khan*. This Hazrat Inayat Khan was an artist, a musician, who taught: introduce the theme, develop it, and end it beautifully.

So naturally when I went to pull the stories out of context, I was so careful to leave the nuggets in the settings. But just as you might want to feel the jewel in the palm of your hand, our editor severed the jewels from the settings; and I approve and applaud his work; also that of the illustrators, Khabir Kitz and Barkat Curtin, whose drawings reflect light on the stories. Finally, Pir Vilayat's mobile introduction leaps and dances with glee, something for all with eyes to see, and then dive in.

MANSUR JOHNSON

Hull, Massachusetts
December, 1979

Contents

Editor's Note v

Hazrat Inayat Khan vii

Introduction xxi

PART ONE: TEACHING TALES

Prayer 1

One Sigh 2

Not Enough 3

Ayaz 7

Tansen's Teacher 10

Shivaji 12

After Death? 14

The Bowl of the Dervish 15

Sarmad 16

Hafiz Shirazi 17

Mira Bai 18

Riches 21

Kindness 22

The Thief 23
Lahu and Kalanki 24
Sa'adi 26
Shirvan Bhagat 27
Farabi 29
The Power of a Word 30
One Word of the King 31
Not Eating Dates 32
Krishna and the Gopis 33
Alif 34
Robbers 37
Evolution 38
Enthusiasm 39
Make God a Reality 40
Animal Nature 42
Shirin and Farhad 43
It Will Go Downward 49

Rabia 51
Firdausi 52
Muhammad Ghauth 53
The Chief Vampire 54
The King's Secret 55
Birbal Asked 56
The Sense of Honor 57
Bayazid's Pilgrimage 58
The King of Balkh 59
Saint Alias 61
In the Form of a Man 62
Where My Murshid Is 63
Uwais 65
Awake 67
The Privilege of Being Human 68
Abd al-Qadir Jilani 70
Sabzpari and Gulfam 72

Shah Khamush 75
Influence 76
Power 77
Reincarnation 78
Tansen Salutes 80
Khidr 81
The Magician 84
The Father's Message 85
A Witty Answer 91
God in All 92
The Occult Laws 94
Beauty 95
Yusuf and Zuleikha 97
Solomon 103
Timurlenk 104
Surdas 106
Usman Haruni 110

Sin and Virtue 112
Honesty 114
Anger 115
In the Mirror 116
Balance 117
Ego Always Wants 118
Two Black Marks 119
The Power of Trust 120
True Faith 122
The Magic Wand 123
Zeb-un-nisa 124
Umar 126
Discrimination 127
Iblis 128
Rustam 129
Haris Chandra 131
A Shah of Persia 133

Hakim 134
The Servant 135
Shigrakavi 136
The Fearless One 138
Laws 139
Wise Love 141
Meditation 142
The Hereafter 144
Leila and Majnun 145
Puran Bhagat 158
The Fire of Love 159
The Tree That Bears All Fruit 161
Tawajjeh 163

PART TWO: EXPERIENCES AND ENCOUNTERS

Spirits I....................167

Spirits II....................169

An Exceptional Dog....................171

A Majdhub in Baroda....................172

Interest and Indifference....................173

A Little Lower....................174

Constancy.................... 175

The Secret....................176

Politeness.................... 177

A Sentence....................178

A Telegraph Clerk....................179

The Turban....................180

Indifference as Love....................181

Music Therapy?....................182

In the Smoke....................183

Muhammad Chehl....184
Mastery....186
A Little Food....187
Memory....189
Spiritual Education....190
Acknowledging....191
Faith....192
Perfect Relief....193
Whom do You Torture?....194
My Murshid's Servant....195
The Vision of My Murshid....196
Gold-Embroidered Slippers....197
Rhythm....198
Bijili....199
The Ideal Life....202
His Life's Purpose....204

Everywhere....205

A Thought of God....206

Recognizing God....207

The Emperors....208

The Tomb of Miran Datar....210

The Sage's Laughter....212

Seeing....213

A Bad Night....215

A Judge in Hyderabad....217

The Appointed Time....218

Mass Belief....219

Living Teaching....220

The Path to Success....221

Forgetting Oneself....222

Duty....223

Luther Burbank....224

No Division....226
Mr. Ford....227
A Warning....228
The Childish Attitude....229
Suddenly....230
Imagination....231
Silence....232
A Child's Question....233
Resist Not Evil....234
Not Acknowledging....235
The Doctor Died....236
Neuritis....237
The Opera....238
Red Walls....239
The Kaiser's Palace....240
Inner Peace....241

A Little Indifference....242
The Man in the Street....243
The Horizon....245
The Doors of Hearing....246
Dig Deep....247
Your Servant, Sir....248
Patience....249
A Faithful Friend....250
Impossible....252
Eternal Matter....254
Mental Illness....255
A Wise Man....256
Freedom....257
Enough....258
Paderewski....259
The End of the World....261

INTRODUCTION
by
Pir Vilayat Inayat Khan

From time immemorial young and old folk alike have sat enthralled by yarns spun by the witty and the wise. Many a kingly court has been brightened by the verve of a jester from distant lands or a troubadour armed with a lute telling tales of prowess more fanciful than real, lifting the spirit into worlds that spell a flight from the humdrum.

Identifying with heroes frees us from our sense of inadequacy, and the fantastic gives us a chance to evade boredom.

Some children will refuse to go to sleep unless transported into fairyland (today it's often the world of television characters) by a benevolent storyteller, usually the mother these days. In older times this was the father's opportunity to communicate with his children in a way that fed his authoritative pride: here was a means of inculcating wisdom and maybe ethics without being too pragmatic, without moralizing. The story fills the child with delight; now, as tension mounts while the tale reaches its exciting denouement, here is the perfect opportunity to point out the inevitable moral lesson—as in the fables of La Fontaine, the jataka tales, Maeterlinck's *Blue Bird*, and many more.

A story is a wonderful opportunity for a teacher to illustrate a point in a practical, tangible way, and to reach his pupils in their everyday lives. Jesus resorted to allegory when he realized his fellows' incapacity to follow the lofty flight of his soul. So did

Mevlana Jalal ad-din Rumi. In fact most Sufis speak in an idyllic rather than idiomatic lore which has the ability of communicating wider ranges of thinking. How can one say that which defies not only our language but our logic except by resorting to metaphor? Hence many a story has added luster to talks given by Sufis to those with blasé minds in search of paradox.

In true oriental style, Hazrat Pir-o-Murshid Inayat Khan's lectures were usually studded with stories, most of them witty. To assess the magic which transpired in his humor one would have to represent him visually—a patriarch conveying an impression of the divine majesty, a mystical yet jovial host—as indeed I remember him when I sat on his lap as he told us children stories. No doubt so intimate a family scene goes beyond the usual confines of experience. But eyewitnesses confirm just how warm and endearing Murshid was when conveying the color, style, and mood of a now almost bygone East.

We owe a debt of gratitude to Mansur Johnson for having collected this garland of stories from the very extensive texts left by Hazrat Pir-o-Murshid Inayat Khan.

Part One

Teaching
Tales

Prayer

There is a well-known story in India of a girl crossing a place where a Muslim was performing his prayers; and the law is that no one should cross where a person is praying.

When the girl returned, the man said to her, "How insolent! Do you know what you have done?"

"What did I do?" asked the girl. And the man told her.

"I did not mean any harm," said the girl. "But tell me, what do you mean by praying?"

"For me, prayer is thinking of God," said the man.

"Oh!" she said. "I was going to see my young man, and I was thinking of him and I did not see you; but if you were thinking of God, how did you see me?"

One Sigh

There is a story of an Arab who was running to the mosque where the prayer of God was being offered, but before he arrived the prayers were finished.

On his way he met a man coming from the mosque, and asked him, "Are the prayers finished?" The man replied that they were finished, and the other sighed deeply and said, "Alas!"

Then the man asked, "Will you give me the virtue of your sigh in exchange for the virtue of my prayers?" And the other agreed.

Next day the simple man saw the Prophet in a dream, who told him that he had made a bad bargain, for that one sigh was worth all the prayers of a lifetime, because it was from the heart.

Not Enough

There was once a young man who was the son of a famous teacher. This teacher had a number of pupils from all over India. Not only was he a very great teacher himself, but he had trained many other teachers; in fact in nearly every village and town there was by now a teacher who had been one of his disciples. Of course this son of his had received all kinds of attention.

Now the son when still a boy one day had a dream, and in this dream he saw himself visiting all the saints. He dreamt that there was a great gathering of saints and spiritual teachers and masters. He was accompanying his father, but whereas his father was admitted to the gathering, he himself was not allowed in.

He felt this as a severe humiliation, so when he woke up next morning he went to his father and said, "I have had a very unhappy vision, for although I went with you to this gathering, you were allowed in and I was not!"

His father replied, "This is a true message for you. To

enter the spiritual path it is not enough for you to be my son; it is necessary for you to become someone's disciple. You have to learn what discipleship means.''

But the son kept thinking to himself, ''I am the son of a great teacher; from childhood I have learned so many things. I have inherited my father's knowledge. However great any teacher was, yet when he met my father he paid him such respect, such great respect. There cannot be anything better in these teachers than there is in me.''

So he thought he should stay with his father and said, ''Can there be anyone better than you, Father, that I should become someone else's disciple?''

But his father answered, ''No, I am no use for that. You must have some other person who is suitable for this purpose.''

''Who?'' asked the young man.

The teacher replied, ''That pupil of mine who was a peasant and who is teaching among peasants. Go to him and be initiated by him.''

The son was very surprised, for he knew that this teacher was not well educated. He was illiterate; he was not of high birth; he had no special reputation; he was not famous in any way. He was just living in a village in humble guise. For all that, his father sent him there.

So he travelled on foot, not very willingly, till he came to the village where this peasant lived. It so happened that this man was on his way on horseback from his own farm to another, and he saw the young man coming towards him.

When the young man came near and bowed before him the teacher looked down on him and said, "Not enough."

Thereupon the young man bowed to his knees.

The peasant teacher again said, "Not enough."

Then he bowed down to his feet, and still the teacher said, "Not enough."

So he bowed down to the horse's knees, but again the teacher said, "Not enough."

So the young man bowed once more, this time to the horse's feet, touching the horse's hoof. Whereupon the peasant teacher said to him, "You can go back now; you have had your training."

That was all! No exercises, no sacred word to learn, nothing to study, no training course. He had learned the lesson he had to learn. It was for this that he had come, a lesson which his father could not give him. So now he was admitted to the circle of the mystics.

Ayaz

There is a story of a slave called Ayaz, who was brought before a king with nine others; and the king had to select one to be his personal attendant.

The wise king gave into the hands of each of the ten a wineglass and commanded him to throw it down. Each one obeyed the command.

Then the king asked each one of them, "Why did you do such a thing?"

The first nine answered, "Because Your Majesty gave me the order": the plain truth, cut and dried.

And then came the tenth slave, Ayaz. He said, "Pardon, Sire, I am sorry," for he realized that the king already knew it was his command; in the reply "Because you told me," nothing new was said to the king. This beauty of expression enchanted the king so much that he selected him to be his attendant.

It was not long before Ayaz won the trust and confidence of the king, who gave him the charge of his treasury, the treasury in which precious jewels were kept.

This sudden rise from slave to treasurer of the king, an envied position, made many jealous. No sooner did people know that Ayaz had become a favorite of the king than they began to tell numerous stories about him in order to bring him into disfavor.

One of the stories was that Ayaz went every day into the room where the jewels were locked in the safe, and that he was stealing them little by little. The king answered, "No, I cannot believe such a thing. You have to show me."

So they brought the king as Ayaz entered this room, and had him stand in a place where there was a hole looking into the room. And the king saw what was going on there.

Ayaz entered the room and opened the door of the safe. And what did he take out from it? His old, ragged clothes which he had worn as a slave. He kissed them and pressed them to his eyes, and put them on the table. There incense was burning, and what he was doing was something sacred to him.

He then put on these clothes and looked at himself in the mirror and said, as one might say a prayer, "Listen, O Ayaz, see what you used to be before. It is the king who has made you, who has given you the charge of this treasure. So regard this duty as your most sacred trust, and this honor as your privilege and as a token of the love and kindness of the king. Know that it is not your worthiness that has brought you to this position. Know that it is his greatness, his goodness, his generosity which has overlooked your faults, and which has bestowed that rank and position upon you by which you are now being honored. Never forget, therefore, your first day, the day when you came to this town; for it is the remembering of that day which will keep you in your proper place."

He then took off the clothes and put them in the same place of safety and came out. As he stepped out, what did he see? He saw that the king before whom he bowed was waiting eagerly to embrace him; and the king said to him, "What a lesson you have given me, Ayaz! It is this lesson which we all must learn, whatever be our position. For before that King in whose presence we are all but slaves, nothing should make us forget that helplessness through which we were reared and raised and brought to life, to understand and to live a life of joy. People told me that you had stolen jewels from our treasure house, but on coming here I have found that you have stolen my heart."

Tansen's Teacher

There is a story of Tansen, the great musician at the court of Akbar.

The emperor asked him, "Tell me, O great musician, who was your teacher?"

He replied, "Your Majesty, my teacher is a very great musician, but more than that. I cannot call him 'musician'; I must call him 'music.'"

The emperor asked, "Can I hear him sing?"

Tansen answered, "Perhaps, I may try. But you cannot think of calling him here to the court."

The emperor said, "Can I go to where he is?"

The musician said, "His pride may revolt even there, thinking that he is to sing before a king."

Akbar said, "Shall I go as your servant?"

Tansen answered, "Yes, there is hope then." So both of them went up into the Himalayas, into the high mountains where the sage had his temple of music in a cave, living with nature, in tune with the Infinite.

When they arrived, the musician was on horseback and Akbar walking. The sage saw that the emperor had humbled himself to come hear his music, and he was willing to sing for him; and when he felt in the mood for singing, he sang. And his singing was great. It was a psychic phenomenon and nothing else. It seemed as if all the trees and plants of the forest were vibrating; it was a song of the universe.

The deep impression made upon Akbar and Tansen was more than they could stand. They went into a state of trance, of rest, of peace. And while they were in that state, the master left the cave. When they opened their eyes he was not there. The emperor said, "Oh, what a strange phenomenon! But where has the master gone?"

Tansen said, "You will never see him in this cave again, for once a man has got a taste of this, he will pursue it, even if it costs him his life. It is greater than anything in life."

When they were home again the emperor asked the musician one day, "Tell me what raga, what mode did your master sing?" Tansen told him the name of the raga, and sang it for him. But the emperor was not content, saying, "Yes, it is the same music, but it is not the same spirit. Why is this?"

The musician replied, "The reason is this, that while I sing before you, the emperor of this country, my master sings before God; that is the difference."

Shivaji

There is an account in the history of India of the life of Shivaji. He was a young robber who used to attack travellers passing along the way where he lived, and he robbed from them whatever he could.

One day before going to his work he came to a sage and greeted him and said, "Sage, I want your blessing, your help in my occupation." The sage asked what his occupation was. He said, "I am an unimportant robber." The sage said, "Yes, you have my blessing."

The robber was very pleased, and went away and had greater success than before. Happy with his success, he returned to the sage. He greeted him by touching his feet and said, "What a wonderful blessing it is to be so successful."

But the sage said, "I am not yet satisfied with your success, I want you to be more successful. Find three or four more robbers and join together, and then go on with your work." So he joined with four or five other robbers who went with him, and again had great success.

Once more he came to the sage and said, "I want your blessing." The sage said, "You have it. But still I am not satisfied. Four robbers are very few. You ought to form a gang of twenty." So he found twenty robbers. And eventually there were hundreds of them.

Then the sage said, "I am not satisfied with the little work you do. You are a small army of young men. You ought to do something great. Why not attack the Moghul strongholds and push them out, so that in this country we may reign ourselves?"

And so he did, and a kingdom was established. The next move of the robber would have been to form an empire of the whole country. But he died. Had he lived, Shivaji would have formed an empire.

The sage could have said, "What a bad thing, what a wicked thing you are doing. Go to the factory and work!" But the sage saw what Shivaji was capable of. Robbery was his first lesson, his ABC. He had only a few steps to advance to be the defender of his country, and the sage realized that he was going to be a king, to release his people from the Moghuls. The robbers did not see it. The young man did not think about it. He was pushed into it by the sage. The sage was not pushing him into robbery; he was preparing him for a great work.

After Death?

Someone went to a Sufi with a question. He said, "I have been puzzling for many, many years and reading books, and I have not been able to find a definite answer. Tell me, what happens after death?"

The Sufi said, "Please ask this question of someone who will die. I am going to live."

The Bowl of the Dervish

Once a dervish came to Sikander, the great king, with the bowl of a beggar, and asked Sikander if he could fill the bowl.

Sikander looked at him and said, "What is he asking of an emperor like me? To fill this little bowl?" He said immediately, "Yes."

But the bowl was a magic bowl. Hundreds and thousands and millions were poured into it, but it would not fill; it always remained half empty, its mouth wide open to be filled.

When Sikander began to feel poor in filling this bowl, he said, "Dervish, tell me if you are not a magician. You have brought a bowl of magic. It has swallowed all my treasures, and it is empty still."

The dervish answered, "Sikander, if the whole world's treasure was put into it, it would still remain empty. Do you know what this bowl is? This is the want of men."

Sarmad

Sarmad, a great Sufi saint who lived in Gwalior, was asked by the emperor Aurangzeb to attend the mosque. For it was against the rules of the time that anyone keep away from the regular prayers which took place in the mosque of the state.

Sarmad, being a man of ecstasy, living every moment of his day and night in union with God, being God-conscious himself, perhaps forgot or refused. A certain time of prayer or a certain place for prayer to him was nothing. Every place to him was a place of prayer; every time was a time of prayer; his every breath was a prayer.

As he refused to attend prayers he was beheaded for breaking the rules which were made for everyone. The consequence was that the Moghul Empire declined, and its downfall can be dated from that time. The entire Moghul civilization, unique in its period, fell to pieces.

Hafiz Shirazi

There is a story told of Hafiz Shirazi, who, together with ten others named Hafiz, was being trained under the same murshid.

A certain time was set apart for their meditation and other practices, and a certain time for food and sleep. Hafiz Shirazi kept awake during the night in rapt contemplation of Allah.

After years of patient waiting, one evening the murshid in ecstasy called for Hafiz. The wakeful Hafiz was the only one who heard, and he answered the call and was blessed by the murshid, who chose this ideal time to inspire all his mureeds.

Each time he called for Hafiz, the same Hafiz answered the call, all the others being asleep. So the wakeful one received an elevenfold blessing, his own and those of the ten others who lost this precious opportunity by their sleep.

And Hafiz became the greatest spiritual healer of his time, whose every word, from that day to this, has been powerful to heal.

Mira Bai

Mira Bai was married to the raja of Udaipur, but soon her tastes in life developed very differently from his. He, always given to the pleasures of hunting and shooting, to the giving of great entertainments, to shows of dancing and acting, began shortly after his marriage to be irritated and vexed by the attitude of Mira Bai towards his amusements. For she was not really interested in any of these things and gradually ceased to show any delight in them; and her mind began to be attracted to quite other aspects of life, to considering the lot of her servants and of the poor in the kingdom, and to philosophy and poetry.

At last the raja, in unreasonable anger at her growing absorption in thoughts and questions that were foreign to his nature, refused to see her or to treat her with the dignity due to her in his court.

Mira Bai took those insults calmly and patiently, with her accustomed sweetness and gentleness, and withdrew to a temple, where she began to devote herself entirely to the study of philosophy and religion, and to the care of the poor and

unfortunate.

The beauty of her hymns of praise, the music of the poetry that she composed and sang in her worship of the Divine, became gradually famed throughout the kingdom of Udaipur; and on account of her great piety and learning many were drawn to the temple where she dwelt. At length her fame reached the court of the emperor Akbar; and he, entirely won by the thoughts and the sweet verses of her songs that were repeated to him, decided that he himself would make a pilgrimage to see her.

And so, both in the guise of beggars, he set out with

Tansen, the divinely inspired musician, learned in the mystery of sound as was Orpheus among the Greeks. After they had entered the temple unknown to anyone and had heard Mira Bai, so moved were they by her music and poetry that Akbar with gratitude and veneration presented to her a most precious necklace. And this necklace Mira Bai took and hung round the neck of the idol of Krishna in the temple, regarded by her as the symbol of the Most Divine.

After that the precious necklace was seen by everyone in the temple, and gradually it became clear that it was Akbar himself who had given it.

When the raja of Udaipur heard of his visit and this gift he felt deeply insulted, and in great anger ordered Mira Bai to leave his kingdom.

So she left the temple and his kingdom and went to Dwarka, where she spent the remainder of her life in seclusion; and from there her fame spread to the boundaries of the empire, and her hymns became loved and were sung not only by her own people but by all the peoples of India.

Riches

When the hermit Machandra said to Gaurikha on their journey through the wilderness, "Gaurikha, I feel afraid," Gaurikha answered, "Throw away the fear."

Machandra answered, "How can fear be thrown away?"

Gaurikha said, "Throw away that which causes you fear."

Machandra took out from his wallet two bricks of gold and said, "These bricks of gold, must I throw them away?"

"Yes," said Gaurikha, "what is it?"

Machandra threw them away, and as he went on his face turned pale.

Gaurikha looked at him and said, "Why are you sad?"

Machandra said, "Now we have nothing."

Gaurikha said, "We have everything. Look before you, what do you behold?" And he beheld mountains of gold.

Gaurikha said, "Take as much as you can, if that is your soul's striving."

Machandra's soul awoke, and he said, "Nothing will I take, for I know the riches of possessing nothing."

Kindness

A story is told in India of an Afghan soldier, who was once travelling with a Brahman. The Brahman, who was a mild and harmless man, careful not to injure the smallest of God's creation, was repeating to himself the word *daya*, which means "kindness."

The Afghan, who was a warrior and understood only the rough side of life, asked him what the word meant. The Brahman explained that the word was the same as *rahm* in his language.

"Ah!" he exclaimed. "I understand very well now what it means. I remember I was kind once in my life, for on the field of battle I saw a wounded man writhing in agony. I was touched and I put my dagger through him and ended his suffering."

The Thief

There is an amusing story of an opium eater who, half asleep, half awake, was lying on the grass with his hat on his knees, thinking, "Suppose a thief came along, what would I do?"

And no sooner had he thought this than he saw a thief before him. He looked for a stick, and he struck the thief hard, whereupon he woke up suddenly and said, "Well, you gave it to me, but I gave it you back all right!"

There was no thief; it was his own knee. His knee with his hat on it appeared for the moment to be a thief because the thought of a thief was in his mind. He gently, slowly raised his stick, and when he struck he never thought that he would strike himself. In this moment there was fear, there was a thief, there was a fight, and there was a hurt; and what was it all? He himself.

Lahu and Kalanki

It is said in the Puranas that once Sita, the consort of Ramachandra, was staying in the guardianship of Vashista Rishi with her sons.

The younger son, Lahu, one day went to see the neighboring town. He saw Kalanki, a most beautiful horse, running about the city without a rider. When he enquired whose the horse was, people told him that this horse had been let loose so that whoever was able to catch it should be made the king of that kingdom.

This tempted the youth, and he ran after the horse in order to catch it. He continued running a long time, and met with nothing but disappointment. Every time he came close to the horse, thinking now he would catch it, it slipped from his hand.

When he reached the point of utter disappointment, he saw his brother coming in search of him, sent by his mother, and he told him that he would not come back till he had caught the horse. The brother said, "That is not the way to catch a horse. In this way you will perhaps run forever and will not be able to catch it. Therefore, instead of running after the horse, run to meet it."

This caused the younger brother to succeed in a moment's time. Then both brothers were taken to the presence of Ramachandra, their father, who embraced both, acknowledging the guidance of the one and the achievement of the other.

Sa'adi

Sa'adi writes in the account of his life: "Once I had no shoes and I had to walk barefoot in the hot sand, and I thought how very miserable I was. And then I met a man who was lame, for whom walking was very difficult. I bowed down at once to heaven and offered thanks that I was much better off than he, who had not even feet to walk upon."

One day Sa'adi was sitting in a bookseller's shop, where his books were sold. The bookseller was absent, and someone came in and asked for one of Sa'adi's books, not knowing that he was speaking to the poet himself.

Sa'adi said, "What do you like about Sa'adi's books?"

He replied, "Oh, he is a funny fellow!"

Whereupon Sa'adi made him a present of the book, and when he wished to pay for it said, "No, I am Sa'adi, and when you called me a funny fellow, you gave me all the reward I could wish for!"

Shirvan Bhagat

There is a well-known story of Shirvan Bhagat. He was devoted to his parents, who had reached the age when they were helpless and entirely dependent upon the service of their only son. Shirvan was so devoted to them that he sacrificed all freedom and pleasure in life in their service. He gently attended to their calls, and bore with patience all the difficulties that one finds in association with the aged.

The parents one day said that they greatly wished they had once in their lives made a pilgrimage to Kashi. This worthy son at once consented to their wish, and, as in those days there was no other means of travelling, he undertook to accomplish the journey on foot. He made baskets in which he placed his old parents, and he lifted them onto his back. And thus he set out on a journey of thousands of miles, through many forests and mountains, crossing rivers on his way.

He travelled for months in this way, but before he arrived at the destination a misfortune happened.

Shirvan, at his parents' request, set down his baskets on the ground and went to fetch some water. When he drew near to the river he was struck by the arrow of Raja Dasheratha, who had aimed at a deer and by accident hit him. Hearing the deep sigh of a man, the raja went to him, and was grieved beyond expression. He said, "Is there anything that I can do for you, O man?"

Shirvan said, "I am dying. I have only one desire, and that is to give my parents this water; they are thirsty in the heat of the sun."

"That is all?" the raja asked. "I will do it with great pleasure as my first duty."

Shirvan said, "If you wish to do anything more, then look after them and see that they are carried to Kashi. Although I doubt whether they will live any longer after I am gone."

The raja went, bearing water in his hands. He gave it to the old parents without saying a word to them, fearing they might not drink it, hearing the voice of a stranger. The parents said, "O worthy son, all our life we have never seen you vexed. This is the first time that you handed us the bowl of water without your loving word, which always gives us new life."

Raja Dasheratha burst into tears and told them of the death of their son. Hearing this, they could not live to drink the water. They lived only on the love of their son. Each of them heaved a deep sigh, "Oh, our beloved Shirvan," and passed away.

This story has since become a tradition in India, and there are followers of this tradition who carry baskets on their shoulders and travel about, teaching the virtue of devotion and service to parents.

Farabi

There is a story known in the East of Farabi, the great singer, who was invited to the court of the emir of Bukhara. The emir welcomed him very warmly at the court, and as the singer entered went to the door to receive him. On coming into the throne room, the emir asked him to take a seat.

"But where shall I sit?" said the singer.

"Sit," the emir said, "in any place that may seem fitting to you."

On hearing this, Farabi took the seat of the king. No doubt this astonished the emir very much, but after hearing the singer's art he felt that even his own seat was not fitting. For he understood that his kingdom had a certain limitation, whereas the kingdom of the artist is wherever beauty prevails. As beauty is everywhere, so the kingdom of the artist is everywhere.

The Power of a Word

There is a story told that once a Sufi was healing a child that was ill. He was repeating a few words, and then gave the child to the parents saying, "Now he will be well."

Someone who was antagonistic to this said to him, "How can it be possible that by a few words spoken, anyone can be healed?"

From a mild Sufi an angry answer is never expected, but this time he turned to the man and said, "You understand nothing about it. You are a fool."

The man was very much offended. His face was red. He was hot. The Sufi said, "When a word has the power to make you hot and angry, why should not a word have the power to heal?"

One Word of the King

There is a story which tells that four persons were arrested for the same crime and were taken before a wise king to be judged.

He saw the first person and said, "Hang him."

He saw the next person and sentenced him for his whole life.

He saw the third person and said, "He must be sent out of the country."

He saw the fourth person and said, "I could never have expected you to do such a crime."

The first three underwent their punishments, but this last one went home. The next morning he was found dead: that one word of the king was worse than death to him.

Not Eating Dates

The Holy Prophet Muhammad was once requested by an aged woman to speak to her son, who spent all his daily wage on dates, leaving her penniless. The Prophet promised to do so after five weeks' interval.

On the appointed day the boy was brought before the Prophet, who spoke to him very kindly, saying, "You are such a sensible lad that you ought to remember that your mother has endured much suffering for your sake, sacrificing all her wages in order to bring you up; and now she is so old and you are in a position to support her, you are squandering your money on dates. Is this just or right? I hope, by the grace and mercy of Allah, you will give up this habit." The boy listened very attentively and profited by what he heard.

The disciples of the Prophet wondered and asked why the reproof was delayed for thirty-five days. The Holy Prophet explained, saying, "I myself am fond of dates, and I felt as if I had no right to advise the lad to abstain from them until I had myself refrained from eating them for five weeks."

Krishna and the Gopis

The legend of the dance of Krishna with a thousand gopis tells that he was beloved of all who knew him. In his village, high and low, young and old held him in their hearts with admiration and friendship.

And each peasant girl, each gopi who saw the divine youth hoped that it would be with her that he would dance. And so one asked him, and another, and another, and to each he gave his promise.

And at the full moon, at the appointed time of the dance, there assembled all the peasant girls or gopis. And then it was that the gentle Krishna seemed to cause a miracle to happen: for each peasant girl danced and believed that it was with her that he danced.

Alif

In the life of Bullah Shah, the great saint of Punjab, one reads a most instructive account of his early training, when he was sent to school with boys of his own age. The teacher taught him *alif*, the first letter of the Arabic alphabet. The other boys in his class finished the whole alphabet while he was mastering the same letter. When weeks had passed, and the teacher saw that the child did not advance any further than the first letter, alif, he thought that he must be deficient. He sent him home to his parents, saying, "Your boy is deficient; I cannot teach him."

The parents did all in their power for him, placing him under the tuition of various teachers, but he made no progress. They were disapponted, and the boy in the end escaped from home so that he should no longer be a burden to his own people.

He then lived in the forest and saw the manifestation of alif which had taken form in the forest as the grass, the leaf, the tree, branch, fruit, and flower. And the same alif was manifested as the mountain and hill, the stones and rocks;

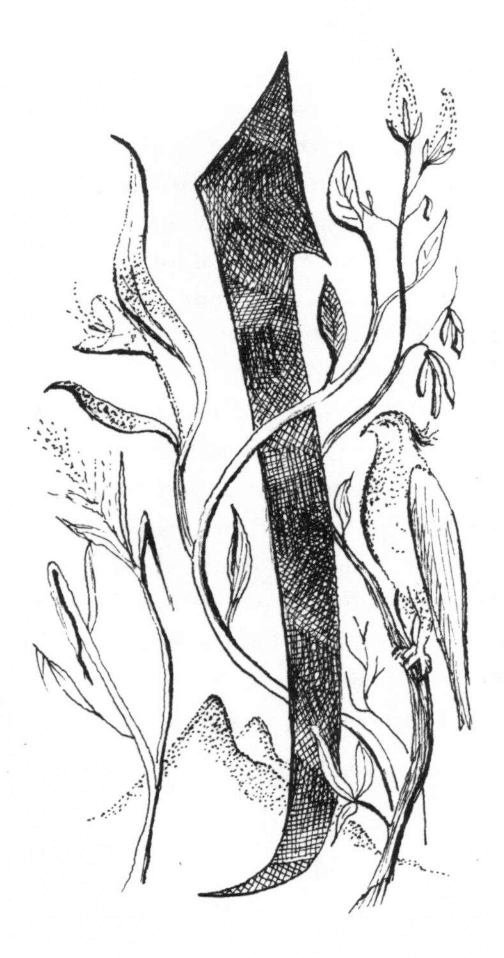

and he witnessed the same as a germ, insect, bird, and beast, and the same alif in himself and others. He thought of one, saw one, felt one, realized one, and none else besides.

After mastering this lesson thoroughly, he returned to pay his respects to his old teacher who had expelled him from school. The teacher, absorbed in the vision of variety, had long ago forgotten him; but Bullah Shah could not forget his old teacher who had taught him his first and most inspiring lesson which had occupied almost all his life. He bowed most humbly before the teacher and said, "I have prepared the lesson you so kindly taught me; will you teach me anything more there may be to learn?"

The teacher laughed at him and thought to himself, "After all this time this simpleton has remembered me."

Bullah Shah asked permission to write the lesson, and the teacher replied in jest, "Write on this wall." Bullah Shah made the sign of alif on the wall, and it divided into two parts.

The teacher was astounded at this wonderful miracle and said, "Thou art my teacher! That which thou hast learnt in the one letter alif, I have not been able to master with all my learning." Bullah Shah sang this song:

Friend now quit thy learning,
One alif is all thou doest need.
By learning thou hast loaded my mind,
With books thou hast filled up thy room.
But the true knowledge was lost by pursuing the false,
So quit now, O friend, the pursuit of thy learning.

Robbers

In ancient times there used to exist communities of robbers, who considered themselves entitled to rob the caravans passing through their territory.

Their morals and principles were such that if one of their victims said, "All I possess I will give you, if you will only let me go," they would say, "No, I wish to see the blood of your hand." They did not let him go without hurting him.

The idea was, as they said, "We do not accept anything from you; we are not beggars, we are robbers. We risk our lives in our profession. We are brave, and therefore we are entitled to do what we do."

It was the same with some of the sea pirates. They believed their profession to be a virtuous one, and from that thought they became kings. The same people, when small, were robbers; but when they became great, they were kings.

Evolution

Moses once passed by a farm and saw a peasant boy talking to himself, saying, "O Lord, Thou art so good and kind that I feel if Thou wert here by me I would take good care of Thee, more than of all my sheep, more than of all my fowls. In the rain I would keep Thee under the roof of my grass shed; when it was cold I would cover Thee with my blanket; and in the heat of the sun I would take Thee to bathe in the brook. I would give Thee bread of manna and would give Thee buttermilk to drink, and to entertain Thee I would sing and dance and play my flute. O Lord my God, if Thou wouldst only listen to this and come and see how I would tend Thee."

Moses was amused to listen to all this, and, as the deliverer of the divine message, he said, "How impertinent on thy part, O boy, to limit the Unlimited One, God, the Lord of hosts, who is beyond form and color and the perception and comprehension of man."

The boy became disheartened and full of fear at what he had done. But immediately a revelation came to Moses:

"We are not pleased with this, O Moses, for We have sent Thee to unite Our separated ones with Us, not to disunite. Speak to everyone according to his evolution."

Enthusiasm

There is a story told in the East of an enthusiastic servant. The master had a headache, and he told the servant to go and fetch some medicine from the chemist. The servant thought it would not be sufficient only to fetch medicine from the chemist, so he also made an appointment with the doctor, and on his way home he visited the undertaker.

The master asked, "Why are you so late?"

The servant said, "Sir, I arranged everything."

Make God a Reality

There was an artist. This artist was devoted to her art; nothing else in the world had attraction for her. She had a studio, and whenever she had a moment to spare her first thought was to go to that studio and to work on a statue she was making.

People could not understand her, for it is not everybody who is devoted to one thing like this. For a time a person interests himself in art, at other times in something else, in the home, in the theater.

But she did not mind. She went every day to her studio and spent most of her time in making this work of art, the only work of art that she made in her life. And the more the work progressed, the more she began to feel delighted with it, attracted by that beauty to which she was devoting her time. And it began to manifest to her eyes, and she began to communicate with that beauty. It was no longer a statue for her, it was a living being.

The moment the statue was finished she could not believe her eyes that it had been made by her. She forgot the work that she had put into the statue and the time that the statue had taken, the thought, the enthusiasm. The world did not exist for her, only this beauty which was produced before her. She could not believe for a moment that this could be a dead statue. She saw there a living beauty, more living than anything else in the world, inspiring and revealing. She felt exalted by the beauty of the statue.

And she was so overcome by the impression that the statue made on her that she knelt down before this perfect vision of beauty with all humility, and asked the statue to speak, forgetting entirely that it was her own work.

And as God is in all things and all beings, as God Himself is all beauty that there is, and as God answers from everywhere if the heart is ready to listen to that answer, and as God is ready to communicate with the soul who is awakened to the beauty of God, there came a voice from the statue: "If you love me, there is only one condition; and that is to take this bowl of poison from my hand. If you wish me to be living, you no more will live. Is it acceptable?"

"Yes," she said. "You are beauty, you are the beloved, you are the one to whom I give all my thought, my admiration, my worship; even my life I will give to you."

"Then take this bowl of poison," said the statue, "that you may no longer be."

For her it was nectar to feel, "I shall now be free from being. That beauty will be, the beauty that I have worshipped and admired will remain. I need no longer be."

She took the bowl of poison and fell dead. The statue lifted her and by kissing her gave her its own life, the life of beauty and sacredness, the life which is everlasting and eternal.

This story is an allegory of the worship of God.

Animal Nature

There is an eastern parable of a dog going to a certain town. His journey was a very long one, taking two or three days as a rule, and yet he arrived before sunset of the same day. The dogs of that town were all surprised to see him so soon.

"Yes, it was a very long journey," the dog said, "but I attribute my speed to the kindness and help of my fellow dogs. Since I left home, whenever I felt tired and tried to stop a moment to rest, four or five would run up and bark at me and want to bite me. So I had to run on without staying to rest in that place, or to search for food. And so it went on at every place I came to, until in the end I have arrived here at my destination."

Shirin and Farhad

Love is never tempted by wealth and grandeur.

Shirin, the daughter of a poor man, but rich in her ideal, was kidnapped and taken to the shah of Fars. He instantly became enamored of her, and gave great rewards to those who had brought her. But to his great disappointment he found that Shirin was unresponsive to his love, and her ideal was too great to allow her to be tempted by the wealth and grandeur of the shah. He did everything to please her and to make her willing to marry him, but every effort had the contrary effect.

At last Shirin saw that there was no hope anywhere of rescue from the palace, which to her was a cage. The importunity of the shah and his servants wore out her patience so much that she was obliged to consent to their offer. She did so on one condition, which was that a canal should be made as a memorial of the occasion.

This was, of course, a pretext for putting off the marriage, for the cutting of the canal was the work of years. The shah was so fascinated by her youth and beauty that he seized upon even the smallest sign of yielding, and at once gave command to the engineers and architects of the court to begin work on a canal without a moment's delay, and to accomplish it as soon as possible, sparing no expense or labor.

Thousands of workmen were soon engaged in this. The work went on night and day unceasingly, under the watchful eye of the king himself and his servants. The nearer the work came to being accomplished, the stronger grew the hope of the king, and he, with great pleasure, requested Shirin to go and look at her canal. With despondent mind, she went to see the canal, fearing that it would soon be finished and she would have to yield to the wishes of the shah, which she regarded as worse than death.

While she was walking, looking at the work going on where thousands of workmen were busy night and day, to her great surprise a workman came up. Won entirely by her beauty and charm, he fearlessly exclaimed, "O Shirin, I love you."

Love overlooks the difference of position of the lover
and the beloved,
And the height that the lover has to climb.

It was that voice of love and that word of devotion that Shirin was looking for and had not found until then. Shirin replied, "Do you love me? Then break these mountains, and cut a pathway through them."

Gold has a test to go through.

Farhad said at once, "Most willingly. Yes, Shirin, whatever you please."

There is nothing too hard for the lover to do for the beloved.

Farhad set out on his journey wholeheartedly, not wondering why he should cut a path, nor reasoning how this great work might be accomplished. He did not stop to think how long it would take to finish, nor had he any misgiving that his efforts might ever be in vain. He went to those mountains in the wilderness and began to break the rocks with his pickax.

He repeated the name of Shirin at every stroke he gave. The strokes of Farhad wrought a miracle. Instead of one stroke it was as if a hundred strokes fell at a time.

Man's power is the strength of his body,
But love's power is the might of God.

No sooner was the work begun than it neared completion. Work that would have taken years with many workers engaged on it was accomplished in days. Shirin had refused the shah since she had seen Farhad, saying, "There is another lover who is undergoing a test, and until I know the outcome of his trial I think it better to keep from marriage."

The king's spies had been watching Farhad from afar, and they immediately sent a report that Farhad had completed his work before the canal was finished. The shah was very much alarmed, thinking that Farhad would most probably win Shirin's love, and that after his having done all this for her, Shirin would not be his.

When he told this to his confidants, one among them said, "Sire, you are the king. Farhad is a workman. What comparison is there between heaven and earth? I will go, if it be the pleasure of Your Majesty, and will finish him in a moment."

"Oh, no," said the shah, "Shirin will see the stain of his blood on me, and will turn her back on me forever."

One among the king's servants said, "It is not difficult for me, My Lord, to bring the life of Farhad to an end without shedding a single drop of blood."

"That is much better," said the shah.

The servant went to Farhad, who had very nearly finished his work, with great hope of a glance from Shirin.

The lover's happiness is in the pleasure of the beloved.

This servant of the shah said, "O Farhad, alas, all is in vain! Oh, that rival of the moon, your beloved Shirin, has passed away by a sudden death."

Farhad said in the greatest bewilderment, "What? Is my Shirin dead?"

"Yes," the servant said, "O Farhad, alas, Shirin is dead."

Farhad heaved a deep sigh and fell to the ground. "Shirin" was the last word that his lips uttered, and made a way for his life to pass away.

Shirin heard from her well-wishers that Farhad had done marvels; that he had cut the path through the mountains repeating the name "Shirin" with his every stroke, and finished the work that might have taken a whole life in the shortest time. Shirin, the chords of whose heart had already been struck by Farhad, and through whose soul the love of Farhad had pierced, had not the patience to rest one moment, and she set out for the mountains at the first opportunity she could find.

The higher powers separate two hearts that come together.

Shirin, who had the great fortune of having a lover like Farhad, had not the fortune to see him anymore. To her greatest grief and disappointment, Shirin found the body of Farhad lying by the side of the wonderful work he had done for her. The spies of the shah came to assure her of his death, hoping that now that Farhad was no more she might fix her mind on the crown of the shah. She only said, "This is poor Farhad. Alas, he is dead."

Shirin heard from the blowing of the wind, from the running of the water, from rocks, from trees the voice of Farhad, calling, "Shirin, Shirin." The whole atmosphere of the place held her soul with the magnetism of love that Farhad had created all around. She fell down, struck by the great loss that her loving heart could no longer sustain, crying, "Farhad, I am coming too, to be with you."

The fate of the lover is a great disappointment in the
sight of the world,
But it is the greatest satisfaction in the eyes of the wise.

It Will Go Downward

To the court of the last emperor of India, Muhammad Shah, a singer came who had invented a new way of composing.

When this man sang his new compositions, he won the admiration and praise of everyone at the court. The singers and musicians were simply amazed to think that there could be a new development in music.

But one of the old musicians who was present said, "If Your Majesty will pardon me I would like to say a word. There is no doubt that this is most beautiful music, and it has won the admiration of all those present, and also my own.

"But I must tell you that from this day the music of the country, instead of going upward will go downward. The music which was handed down to us has weight, it has substance, but now it seems that this has been lost and that the music has become lighter. Therefore from now on it will go downward."

And so it happened; step by step after that music was brought down.

Rabia

There is an account in the story of Rabia, the great Sufi. Once in her vision, she saw the Prophet, and the Prophet asked her, "Rabia, to whom have you given your devotion?"

And Rabia said, "To God."

And the Prophet said, "Not to me?"

And Rabia said, "Yes, Prophet, you include God, but it is God I gave my devotion to."

Firdausi

There was a poet of Persia, Firdausi, who was asked by the king to write the history of the country. The king promised him a gold coin for every verse.

Firdausi went into solitude and wrote down the traditions of centuries; characters, lives, deeds—he saw it all as a play, and he wrote of it in verse.

When he returned to the court, the king was most impressed; he thought it wonderful.

But there are always many in the world who will reject such things. The truth is only accepted by the few. At the court he was much criticized, and many showed skepticism. It went so far that they told the king that it was all Firdausi's imagination.

It hurt him terribly. He took the one who had spoken most against him and held his hand upon his head, and said to him, "Now, close your eyes and look." And what this man saw was like a moving picture and he exclaimed, "I have seen."

But the poet's heart was wounded and he would not accept the gold coins.

Muhammad Ghauth

There was once a well-known dervish in Gwalior, Muhammad Ghauth, who sat in the jungle unclothed and only ate when food was brought to him. He was poverty-stricken in the eyes of the world, but was respected by all.

Evil days came on Gwalior. The state was threatened by a powerful enemy, with an army twice the size of that belonging to the ruler. He in his distress sought Muhammad Ghauth.

The sage at first asked to be left in peace. But his help being further entreated by the maharajah himself, he at last said, "Show me the army that is threatening you."

They took him outside the city and showed him the vast host that was advancing. Muhammad Ghauth waved his hand, repeating the word *maktul* ("be destroyed"). As he did so, the army of the maharajah of Gwalior appeared immense to the oncoming army, which turned in fear and fled.

This Sufi saint was the possessor of the kingdom of heaven. His tomb is now in a palace, and the kings of the earth come and bow before it.

The Chief Vampire

There is a story of the maharajah of Jaipur, that in his kingdom there was a cult of vampires. He sent for the chief of that cult and said, "Can you show some phenomena of your powers?" The wizard said yes.

"Then come on," the maharajah said, "and show something of what you can do." And again he said yes.

Before each one of the vampires, according to their request, one melon was placed, and each looked at the melon for about five minutes. Afterwards the melons were cut, and there was nothing left. There were only the outer rinds: the inner parts were all eaten.

Through the eyes the will power of man goes out as a command which is even stronger than words. The eyes can even be so powerful that they can perform magic.

The King's Secret

It is said that a king gave some secret to his attendant, an undeserving person, for he had no one else to give that secret to.

As soon as the undeserving person had the secret, he became ill. He thought, "I must never give that secret away, but if I keep the secret, I will get ill." He was very uneasy. He could not eat. He could not sleep. He could not do anything since the king had given this secret to him. He was almost mad. What to do?

He went to a wise man and said, "I am dying, I am dying. I want to speak it before somebody. I have such a pain; I am uneasy. If I speak before somebody the king will take my life, and if I keep my life I am ill."

The wise man said, "Go into the forest, far away, and tell the secret to a tree."

And when he went and told the secret to the tree he felt easy, and from then the illness was gone.

Birbal Asked

During the reign of Akbar there lived a great sage in Delhi. One day the emperor heard about him and wanted to go and pay him homage. The sage saw sitting on a rock with legs stretched out and arms folded. The emperor had Birbal, his friend and minister, with him; and the latter did not like the way the emperor was received by this sage, for though the sage knew quite well that it was the emperor, he remained in the same position.

So Birbal asked the sage sarcastically how long he had been sitting in this way. And the answer of the sage was, "Since I folded my hands."

This means, "As long as my hands were held out in need, my legs stood up. But since my hands do not ask for anything anymore, my legs remain stretched out. It makes no difference if a king or emperor comes." In other words, "As long as I had interest, my legs were functioning, but since I have no interest anymore I sit in the way I like to sit."

The Sense of Honor

Once the nizam of Hyderabad was walking in the country, and a knight happened to see a thorn stuck in his shoe. He rushed before the attendant had seen it, and took out that thorn from the king's shoe.

The king looked back and said, "Were there no attendants present? It was for them, not for you. And since you have taken this work, you can no longer continue to be my knight. Please retire."

It is not by the humbleness of the surroundings that the king is exalted; it is the sense of honor expressed by his surroundings that makes a king a true king.

Bayazid's Pilgrimage

Bayazid was going on a pilgrimage to Mecca. A dervish was sitting by the way on his journey. Wanting to pay homage to a spiritual man, he went to the dervish and sat down to receive his blessing.

The dervish asked him, "Where are you going?"

He said, "I am going to Mecca."

"On business?"

He was astonished. "No, on a pilgrimage."

"On a pilgrimage? What do they do on the pilgrimage?"

Bayazid replied, "They walk around the holy stone of Ka'bah."

The dervish said, "You do not need to go so far for that pilgrimage. If you will make circles round me and go back, your pilgrimage is done."

Bayazid said, "Yes, I believe this."

He circled around the man and went back home; and when people asked, "Did you make a pilgrimage to the Ka'bah?" he said, "Yes, I made a pilgrimage to a living Ka'bah."

The King of Balkh

A certain king went to a murshid with a desire to learn from him.

He said, "Will you accept me as one of your disciples? I would so much like to be counted among your humble servants instead of staying any longer on my throne."

The murshid agreed to take him on probation, saying, "Yes, and your first task will be to take the garbage from the house and throw it in a certain place outside the town."

Now every one of the disciples knew that he was a king who had willingly resigned his kingdom; he was not exiled, he did not have to run away from the throne, he had left it willingly. They felt sympathy for him to be tried in this way, and they all said to the murshid in the course of time, "Pray do not expect this task of him any more. He has been doing it for such a long time."

But the answer was, "He is not yet ready for initiation." To one pupil who argued about the matter he said, "Well, you can test him in any way which you think good."

So as he was taking the basket one day, one of the young

men came up beside him and by pushing him upset the contents onto the floor. The king looked at him and then said to him, "Had I still been a king as I was, I would have done to you as a king would. But now, of course, I am not that, so I must not show my temper." With that he gathered all the refuse together and put it back in the basket and took it all away.

This was reported to the murshid, but he said, "Did I not tell you he is not ready yet?"

However, one of the pupils went to the teacher again and asked him to be kind to him and give him another task. But he answered, "Try him again."

So he had to go through the same experience. This time the king said not a word, he only looked at the offender for a moment, and again gathered the refuse together, put it back in the basket and went on his way. When this report too was brought to the murshid, he again said, "Not ready, not ready."

Then the same thing was done a third time. This time the king was not only silent, but took up the garbage without even looking at the person who upset it. And when the murshid heard about this, he answered, "Now he is right; the time has now come."

Saint Alias

There is a story of the great Indian composer Saint Alias. He was an ascetic, and for his daily food a loaf of bread was enough. It happened that people gave him more, but he would never keep anything for tomorrow; he would always give away what he had not eaten that day.

And if one asked him why he made himself dependent upon other people, he would answer, "We are all interdependent. As long as I do not force myself upon others it all comes from God and it all goes to God's creatures."

In the Form of a Man

A very well-known seer went to see Jalal ad-din Rumi when he was a chief judge in the city of Kazi. It was Shams ad-din Tabrizi. He came before the judge in the appearance of a savage.

The first thing he did in coming before him was to throw his manuscripts into the pond. Rumi looked at him, wondering about his action and why he should throw away all that knowledge, and asked him the reason for his action.

The seeming vagrant said, "Because you have been reading all your life, and now you should do something more. You ought to understand what you are, and where you are. Everything before you is made of letters. If you could read them, then you could read life, and it would be greater than any scripture, better than any tradition that you can hear. It would disclose the secret of all being."

Rumi, after having looked at this person and his expression, and having heard all he said, was so won by him that he wrote down in his diary, "The God whom I have been worshipping all my life has today appeared to me in the form of a man."

Where My Murshid Is

There is a story of a mureed who was known to be a great devotee of his murshid. After the death of his teacher a great sage came to that village where he lived, and people began to say all around the village that so great was the power of this sage that coming in his presence would make a person liberated from all his sins.

This man, who was most spiritually inclined, was the first expected to visit this sage. But everybody from the village came to greet the sage except this one. They were all wondering why it was so: that man who was really deep in the idea was the very man who had not come.

So the sage went himself there, and asked this young man, "What was the matter that you did not come to see me? Everyone talked about you, and I was eager to make your acquaintance. Is there any antipathy you have for me, or what is it?"

He said, "No, I would be the last person to have an antipathy towards a spiritual soul like you. But there was one thing that kept me back." In his simple way he said, "People told me that by seeing your holiness I would be liberated from all sins. But I do not know yet where my murshid is going to be, in heaven or in the other place. If, by being liberated, I went to heaven, and if I found that my murshid was in the other place, then that heaven would be hell for me. I would rather be where my murshid is. Even if it were hell, it would become heaven for me.''

Uwais

They say that Muhammad had a friend who had never seen him; he lived at a great distance from the Prophet, in another town. His name was Uwais al-Karani. He always was eager to get news of the Prophet. When the news reached him he would be most happy to hear something about him.

And one day they said that the Prophet was in the war, in battle, and one tooth of the Prophet had come out in the struggle. When the man heard this he said, "One tooth of the Prophet came out! How could I have teeth in my mouth! I feel uncomfortable." And he took out every tooth. "For one tooth of the Prophet I will take out all my teeth!"

Still he would not go to see the Prophet, for one command of the Prophet he was following: "If your parents are old, helpless, dependent upon you, then even sacrifice your privilege of coming to me and serve them." And this command he was obeying.

In the end, before he could reach the Prophet, he died. And when the Prophet was dying, among his millions of followers he thought of Uwais and said, "My mantle must be given to Uwais.''

That remains in history after hundreds of years. One person who never saw the Prophet was always his greatest friend.

Awake

There is a well-known story told among Sufis that Shams ad-din Tabrizi, the Shiva of Persia, was once most respectfully entreated by the priests of the day to awaken the crown prince from his last long sleep. The shah, his father, issued a decree that if there was any truth at all in religion, his only son must be restored to life by prayer. Otherwise, all the mosques should be destroyed and the mullahs be put to the sword. In order to save many lives Shams ad-din complied with their request and sought the dead body of the prince.

He first said to the body of the prince, "Awake at the call of God." The dead body did not move.

He then, under the spell of ecstasy, exclaimed, "Awake at my command." At this suggestion the prince immediately arose.

The story goes on to relate that this abrupt command, although it restored the prince to life, brought the charge of the claim of godhead upon Shams ad-din Tabrizi, and according to the religious law, he was condemned to be flayed alive. He gladly submitted to this punishment in order to keep religion intact, as it was the only means of governing the masses.

The Privilege of Being Human

Why is it so great a privilege to be man? There is a legend which explains this very clearly.

The angels once rebelled against God, saying, "Why should man be made higher than all other creatures? Man has the animal attributes. Man needs to eat; we do not. Man needs to drink; we do not. Man needs to sleep; we do not."

God said, "We will decide this question after a trial." And He said to one of the angels, "Go upon earth and see what man's life is."

The angel flew down to earth. He saw a tree. He was so delighted with the tree that he climbed down upon it and began to eat its fruit. He was so enchanted that he thought, "This is the best place to live. I was a miserable creature when I did not have this."

Then he saw a young girl passing beneath the tree, selling fruit. He was charmed by her beauty and asked her to sell him the fruit. They became friends; they became lovers; they married and had children.

At first the angel was very, very happy; but when the

freshness, the newness went, the charm and the happiness wore away. He began to find that those who had been his friends yesterday were not his friends today, that those who had been kind once were kind no longer. Life became very difficult. All the burdens and cares of life fell upon him. He felt oppressed, suffocated, and he grew very unhappy and complained of his life on earth.

Then God said to another angel, ''Go and see what your brother is doing.'' The angel went down to earth. He too was delighted with the earth, its trees and fruits. But when the other angel told him of his life and all its difficulties and troubles, he flew back, and so was saved from these experiences.

When the angels appeared again before God, God said, ''When even the angels are tempted by the earth and forget Me, should I not be proud of man when he, having all the troubles and difficulties and burdens of life on earth, sometimes remembers Me, thinks of Me?''

Abd al-Qadir Jilani

Abd al-Qadir Jilani, a great Sufi saint, was one day engaged in prayer when in a vision he saw the semblance of an angel, who addressed him, saying, "O thou who hast prayed continuously all thy life, to thee God sends the good tidings that no more prayers are required of thee."

The saint, recognizing the tempter, replied, "Begone, thou wicked one. I recognize thee in spite of thy angelic guise: thou art a devil come to tempt me. All the holy ones have passed their lives in prayer, and how can I deem myself worthy to be exempt from it?"

On hearing these words the evil one vanished.

Sabzpari and Gulfam

Sabzpari, a fairy who was one of the dancers of the court of Indra, the king of heaven, was attracted by Prince Gulfam, a man on earth, while she was flying over his palace. Her servant, the Black Deva, carried Gulfam at her desire from earth to heaven.

Gulfam was at first most unhappy in the strange place, but then the love of Sabzpari attracted him so much that he lived in her love. Sabzpari had to be at the court of Indra every night to dance and entertain him. In the love of Gulfam she was absent a few times, and everyone at the court wondered why she was not there.

But her going nightly to the court made Gulfam suspect that perhaps there might be someone else who was entertained by Sabzpari's charms. He asked her about this many times, and every time she refused to tell him, until he became vexed and Sabzpari thought she could not hide it from him any longer.

On hearing her explanation Gulfam requested her to take him to the court of Indra. She said, "No man has ever been there, no man can ever go there, and if Indra should see thee it would at once end our sweet days of love and happiness. We should surely be separated, and I know not what he would do to thee."

Gulfam said, "No. It is a woman's tale. Thou art perhaps in love with some deva, and wishest to hide it by telling me a story."

Sabzpani was most unhappy, finding herself in a helpless situation. Under the spell of the agony that his arrow-like words had produced in her heart, she consented, without thinking, to take Gulfam to the court of Indra, saying to herself, "What will be, will be."

Sabzpari took him to the court, hiding him behind the folds of her garment and her wings which spread about her. The Red Deva sensed the presence of a man in the court, and, looking all around, he found that Sabzpari was dancing most skillfully before Indra, hiding Gulfam behind her. He humbly brought him before Indra, the lord of the heavens, who was sitting on a throne with a glass of wine in his hand, his eyes red with the wine and his high being full of glory and grandeur.

When Indra saw that a man had been brought into the apex of the heavens, he rose in great wrath and said to Sabzpari, "O shameless one, how darest thou bring a man into the summit of the heavens, where no earthly creature has ever been allowed to come?"

The Red Deva said, "It is her love for this earthly creature, My Lord, that has turned her faithless to the heavenly crown and made her fail in her duty at the supreme court of Your

Majesty.''

Sabzpari said to Gulfam, ''Seest thou, my darling beloved, what has befallen us through thy insistence?''

Indra said, ''Separate them at once, that they may no more speak a word to one another. Throw him back into the depths of the earth, and tear her wings off and keep her captive until the love of Gulfam is wiped from her heart. Then purify the polluted one from the five elements. Then only can she come again, if she be allowed by our favor, forgiveness, and mercy.''

Shah Khamush

In Hyderabad there was a mystic called Shah Khamush. He was called so because of his silence.

In his youth he was a very clever and energetic young man. One day he went to his murshid, and as usual he had some question to ask, as is natural in a pupil.

The murshid was sitting in ecstasy, and as he did not wish to speak he said to him, "Be quiet."

The boy was much struck. He had never before heard such words from his murshid, who was always so kind and patient and willing to answer his questions. But it was a lesson which was enough for his life, for he was an intelligent person.

He went home and did not speak to his family, not even to his parents.

Then his murshid, seeing him like that, did not speak to him anymore.

For many years Shah Khamush never spoke, and his psychic power became so great that it was enough to look at him to be inspired. Wherever he looked, he inspired. Wherever he cast his glance, he healed.

Influence

There is a story about a poor man whose job was to sell empty bottles in Bombay. He came to a merchant and asked a certain salary to do this work for him, and from the day the merchant engaged him he steadily became more prosperous.

So one day he thought, "I have worked for twenty years in this shop, and it is only since this young man has come that I have prospered."

He did not tell this to the young man, but the next day he made him a partner in his business; and from that time he began to flourish a hundred times more.

After six months he was flourishing and prospering in every way, and in the end, as he had no children, he gave his business to this young man, who in time became the wealthiest man in the whole country.

Power

In one of the great wars that the Prophet Muhammad had to fight the whole army was defeated, and there only remained ten or fifteen friends by the side of the Prophet. All the others ran away or were dead or wounded.

Then the Prophet turned to his people and saw that they were all downhearted and despairing. So he said, "Look, before us there is an army and here are we, fifteen men. You do not see any hope; now you must retreat. But I, I will stand here whether I am to come back victorious or lose my life here on the battlefield. Now go. Many have already left, so you go also."

They said, "No, Prophet, if your life is to be ended here on the battlefield, our lives will be taken first. What are our lives after all! We shall give our lives together with you, Prophet. We are not afraid of this enemy."

And then the Prophet threw away the sword he had in his hand and bowed down and took a few pebbles from the earth and threw them at the army. And the army began to run, and ran for miles and miles. They did not know what was behind them. It was only a few pebbles; but what they saw were great missiles, and they ran.

Reincarnation

In support of reincarnation a story is told of two friends who were going out on a holiday. One said, "Let us go to the temple. There we shall hear the name of God, we shall be uplifted."

The other said, "You are always such a melancholy boy; you always find such dull occupations. We will not go to the temple, we will go where we can enjoy ourselves. We will go to the Gaiety."

The first said, "I do not like that idea, I will not go with you." So they parted. The one who went to the temple on the way met with an accident from a wagon on the road, and his foot was crushed. He thought, "What a good thing that my friend did not come with me; he too would have been injured."

The other on his way to the Gaiety had great luck; he found a purse full of gold coins. He thought, "Thank God! If my friend had been with me, I should have had to share this with him!"

As soon as the first had recovered a little, he went to a

Brahman and asked him, "What was the reason that I, who was on my way to the temple, had the bad luck to have my foot crushed, and my friend, who was on his way to the Gaiety, had the good luck to find a gold purse?"

The Brahman said, "The reason is that you in your former life did some very bad action, and you were meant to be killed, and not only killed but hanged for everybody to see. But it happened that only your foot was crushed. Your friend in his former life did some very good action and he was meant to be a king, but it happened for his present sins that he only found a purse full of gold coins."

Tansen Salutes

When Tansen, the great singer, left the court, hurt by a remark of the emperor Akbar, he went to Rewa, a state in central India. When the maharajah of Rewa heard that Tansen was coming he was perplexed, wondering in what way he should honor him.

A chair was sent for Tansen, to bring him to the palace, and when he arrived Tansen expected the maharajah at least to receive him at the door. So as soon as he got out of the chair he said, "Where is the maharajah?" And the man whom he asked replied, "Here is the maharajah!" pointing to the one who had been carrying the chair all through the city.

Tansen was most touched, and he said, "You could not have given me a greater reward." From that day Tansen saluted him with his right hand, saying, "This hand will never salute anyone else all my life."

And so it was. Tansen would not even salute the emperor with his right hand. Such was the appreciation, the acknowledgement of talent in ancient India.

Khidr

There is a story that Moses was passing with Khidr through a country. Khidr was the murshid of Moses when Moses was being prepared for prophethood. Moses was first given the lesson of discipline, to keep quiet under all circumstances. When they were walking through the beauty of nature, the teacher and pupil both were quiet. The teacher was exalted in seeing the beauty of nature; the pupil also felt it. And so they arrived on the bank of a river, where Moses saw a little child drowning, and the mother crying aloud, for she could not help.

And then Moses could not keep his lips closed; he had to break that discipline and say, "Master, save him, the child is drowning!"

The murshid said, "Quiet!"

Moses could not keep quiet. He said again, "Master, Master, save him! The child is drowning!"

Khidr said, "Quiet!" and Moses was quiet. But the mind of Moses was restless; he did not know what to think. "Can the master be so thoughtless, so inconsiderate, so cruel, or is the master powerless?'' he asked himself. He could not understand which was which. He did not dare to think such a thought, and yet it made him very uncomfortable.

As they went further they saw a boat sinking; and Moses said, ''Master, that boat is sinking, it is going down.'' The master again ordered him to be quiet; so then Moses was quiet, but he was still most uncomfortable.

When they arrived home, he said, ''Master, I thought that you would have saved this little innocent child from drowning, and that you would have saved that boat which was going down in the water. But you did nothing. I cannot understand, but I would like to have an explanation.''

The master said, ''What you saw, I saw also. We both saw. So there was no use in your telling me what was happening, for I knew. If I had thought that i- was better to interfere, I could have done it. Why did you take the trouble to tell me, and spoil your vow of silence?''

He continued, "The child who was drowning was going to bring about a conflict between two nations, and thousands and thousands of lives were going to be destroyed in that conflict. When he was drowned, this averted the other danger which was to come." Moses looked at him with great surprise.

Then Khidr said, "That boat that was sinking was a boat of pirates, and was sailing in order to wreck a large ship full of pilgrims, and was then to take what was left in the ship and bring it home. Do you think that you and I can be judge of it? The Judge is behind; He knows His actions, He knows His work. When you were told to be quiet, it was to keep your lips closed and to observe everything silently, as I was doing."

There is a Persian verse which says, "It is the gardener who knows which plant to rear and which to cut down."

The Magician

There was a magician who imagined that he was fluid, liquid, moving, rising and falling, and turning into the sea. Then he imagined, "Now I am solid."

Atoms grouped together, froze and turned into ice; then he thought, "I am not so cold. I can try and be stable, and will not melt," and he turned into stone.

Next he said, "Now I want to change. I do not want to remain stone." And he became a tree. "But," he said, "still I am not moving, not working," and he twisted and moved, and turned into an insect.

But the magician thought, "How helpless it is to live as an insect! I should like to play and sing," and he turned into a bird. Then he said, "I want to be more gross and dense, and feel myself more intelligent," and he turned into an animal. Finally he said, "I want to stand on my hind legs, to stretch my spine," and he turned into man.

This is the phenomenon of a magician who wanted, who imagined something, and who became it.

The Father's Message

There was a man living with his wife and children in a little village. He was called away by the inner voice of his soul, and he renounced his life with his wife and children and went into the wilderness, to a mountain called Sinai, taking with him his eldest son, the only one of his children who was grown up.

The children, having a faint remembrance of their father, wondered at times where he was and longed to see him. They were told by their mother that he had gone away long ago, and perhaps had passed from this earth.

At times in answer to their longing she would say, "Perhaps he will come or send word, for so he promised before his departure."

Sometimes the children grieved at their father's absence, their father's silence. And whenever they felt the need for him to be among them, they would comfort themselves with the hope, "Perhaps someday he will be with us as he has promised."

After some time the mother also passed away, and the children were left with guardians who were entrusted with their care, together with the care of the wealth left by their parents.

Some years later, when their brother's smooth face had become bearded and when his cheerful look had given place to a serious expression and his fair skin, now in the strong sun for years, had turned brown, he came home.

He went away with his father in grandeur; he returned in poverty and knocked at the door. The servants did not recognize him and did not allow him to enter.

His language was changed. The long stay in a foreign country had made him forget all. He said to the children, "Come, O brothers, ye are my father's children. I have come from my father, who is perfectly peaceful and happy in his retirement in the wilderness. He has sent me to bring you his love and his message, that your life may become worthwhile and that you may have the great happiness of meeting your father, who loved you so greatly."

They answered, "How can it be that thou comest from our father who has been gone so long, and has given us no sign?"

He said, "If ye cannot understand, ask your mother. She will be able to tell you."

But the mother had already passed away; only her grave was left, which could never tell.

He said, "Then consult your guardians. Perhaps they will be able to tell you from the recollections of the past; or things that our mother may have said to them might bring to their memory the words of our father about my coming."

The guardians had grown careless, indifferent, blind. They were quite happy in the possession of all the wealth, enjoying the treasured gold left in their charge, and using their undisputed power and complete hold over all the children. Their first thought on hearing he had come was of annoyance; but when they saw him they were quite heedless, for they found in him no trace of what he had been like before. And as they saw he was without power or wealth, and was altered in looks, in dress, in everything, they cared not for him.

They said, "By what authority claimest thou to be the son of our father, of our master, who has long since passed away, and may perhaps be dwelling in the heavens by now?"

Then he said to the children, "I love you, O children of my father, although you cannot recognize me. Even if you do not acknowledge me as your brother, take my helping word for your father's word, and do good in life and avoid evil, for every work has its reward like unto it."

The older ones, who were hardened in their ways, paid no heed, and the little ones were too young to understand. But the middle ones who hearkened to his words followed him quietly, won by his magnetism and charmed by his loving personality.

The guardians became alarmed at the thought that the children in their charge might be tempted and carried off. They thought, "Someday even the remaining ones may be charmed by his magic; and our control over them, the possession of their wealth, our comfort in their home, and our importance and honor in their eyes will all be lost if we let this go on any longer."

They made up their minds to kill him, and incited the remaining brothers against him, declaring before them the pity of their dear brothers being led astray and carried away from their home and comfort, and how unfounded was the claim he made.

They came up to this man and arrested him, and bound his arms and legs and threw him into the sea. But those children who had looked upon him as their guide and brother grieved and lamented at this.

The brother consoled them, saying, "I will come to you again, O children of my father. Do not give up hope. The things that you have not understood, being young, will be taught to you fully. As these people have behaved so harshly towards me, it will be shown them what it is to be heedless of our father's message brought by his own son. And you will be enlightened, O children of my father, with the same light with which I came to help you."

This man was a master swimmer. The sea had no power to drown him. He seemed to them to have sunk, but then he drew his hands and feet out of the knots, rose upon the water and began to swim in a masterly way, as he had been taught.

He went to the father in the wilderness and told him all his experiences on his long journey, and showed his love and desire to obey his father's will and fulfill all his commandments; to go to the children of his father again with renewed strength and power, in order to bring them to that ideal which was the only desire of the father.

A bearer of the message of their father appeared again

after a few years. He did not insist on proving himself to be the son of their father, but tried to guide them and help them towards the ideal set for them by their father.

The guardians, disturbed already by one who came and went, insulted him, stoned him, and drove him out of their sight. But he, renewed in his power, strength and courage, and coming fresh from the mighty influence of his father, withstood it courageously with sword and shield, and sought refuge among those of the brothers who responded to him and sympathized with him on his last coming.

They said, "Surely he who came before was from our father, whom our brothers did not recognize and have sunk in the sea. But we are awaiting his coming, for he promised us that he would come."

He answered, "It is myself who promised, and went to our father, and now I have come back. For the promise given to you was of two natures: 'I will come again' was said to those who could recognize me in a different garb, suited to the time and the situation; and 'I will send another' or 'Another will come' was said to those who were likely to be confused by the external garb. It was said to them so that they might not refuse the word of guidance sent by our most loving father."

They understood his word better, but refused to acknowledge him to be the same as the first, whom they had formerly seen and now expected. He spoke, and he showed in his works the signs of their father, but they clung to the person whom they had seen at first, forgetting his word and their father.

But the little ones, who had not known him before, felt the

tie of the blood relationship, for neither were their hearts hardened nor were they set strongly in their ideas. They loved him, and they recognized him more than at his former coming; while the other brothers, under the influence of the guardians, fought and rebelled against all that this man did.

But in spite of all their resistance and the suffering caused to him, he guided the children of his father, as many as he could, until the name of his father was again glorified and his brothers were guided, directly or indirectly, through the puzzles of the world and the secrets of the heavens.

A Witty Answer

A padishah was once riding in the jungle. Crossing a bridge, he saw a man who was quite drunk standing in the middle of the road.

The man called out, "Will you sell that horse, O passerby?" For he was quite drunk and could not recognize the rider.

The padishah thought, "He is drunk," so he paid no heed. After shooting for some hours in the jungle, he returned, and saw the man who had been standing in the middle of the road now sitting by the roadside. The padishah asked the man in fun, "Do you still want to purchase this horse?"

The man's drunkenness had now passed. He was astonished to think what he had said to the padishah in his drunken state, but fortunately he thought of a very witty answer. He said, "The purchaser of the horse has gone; the groom of the horse remains."

This amused the padishah, who overlooked his fault.

God in All

Moses once begged the Lord God of Israel on Sinai, "O Lord, Thou hast so greatly honored me in making me Thy messenger. If there could be any greater honor I should think it this, that Thou shouldst come to my humble abode and break bread at my table."

The answer came, "Moses, with great pleasure We shall come to thy abode."

Moses prepared a great feast and was waiting eagerly for God to come. There happened to pass by his door a beggar, and he said to Moses, "Moses, I am ill and weary, and I have had no food for three days and am at the point of death. Pray give me a slice of bread and save my life."

Moses, in his eagerness, expecting at every moment a visit from God, said to the beggar, "Wait, O man, thou shalt have more than a slice, plentiful and delicious dishes. I am waiting for a guest who is expected this evening. When he is gone, then all that remains I will give to thee that thou mayest take it home."

The man went away. Time passed on, God did not come,

and Moses was disappointed. Moses went the next day to Sinai and grieved bitterly, saying, "My Lord, I know Thou doest not break Thy promise, but what sin have I, Thy slave, committed that Thou didst not come as Thou hadst promised?"

God said to Moses, "We came, O Moses, but alas, thou didst not recognize Us. Who was the beggar at thy door? Was he other than We? It is We who in all guises live and move in the world, and yet are remote in Our eternal heavens."

The Occult Laws

Once a man went to a Chinese sage and said to him, "I want to learn the occult laws. Will you teach me?"

The sage said, "You have come to ask me to teach you something. But we have so many missionaries in China who come to teach us."

The man said, "We know about God, but I have come to you to ask you about occult laws."

The sage said, "If you know about God you don't need to know anything more. God is all that is to be known. If you know Him you know all."

Beauty

There is a story told in the East of how a king was debating with his philosophers and friends on the question of wherein beauty lies. As they were talking together on the terrace of the palace, they watched their children playing below in the courtyard.

Suddenly the king called to the slave of his courtyard and, handing him a jewelled cap, said, "Now take this and put it on the head of the child whose beauty seems to you to suit it best. Choose and crown the most beautiful of all those playing down there."

The slave, a little embarrassed, but pleased and interested, took the jewelled cap most carefully. First he tried it on the king's son. He saw that it suited the handsome lad, and yet somehow the slave was not quite satisfied: there seemed to him something lacking about the child. He tried it on the head of another and another, till at last he put it on his own little son.

There he saw that the cap fitted his child exactly. It became him wonderfully; it was just the right cap for him. So the slave took his son by the hand and led him to the king. Trembling a little with fear, he said, "Sire, of all the children, I find that the crown suits this one best of all. Indeed, if I tell the truth I must say this, though I am ashamed to appear so bold; for indeed the boy is the son of my most unworthy self."

Then the king and those with him laughed very heartily as he thanked the slave and rewarded him with the same cap for his child, saying, "Certainly you have told me what I wished to know: it is the heart that perceives beauty."

For the son of this slave was indeed a very ugly child, as the king and all those with him saw at a glance.

Yusuf and Zuleikha

From the story of Yusuf and Zuleikha we learn what part beauty plays in the world of love.

Yusuf was the youngest son of Jacob, the seer, who was blessed with the gift of prophecy, as were several among his ancestors.

He was thrown into a well by his elder brothers, who were jealous of his beauty and the influence that it had on their father and everyone that met him.

Not love alone, but beauty also has to pay its forfeit.

Some merchants travelling that way saw Yusuf in the well as they were drawing water. They took him up and sold him as a slave to a chief of Misr, who, charmed by the beautiful manner of this youth, made him his personal attendant.

Zuleikha, the wife of this chief, grew fonder every day of this handsome youth. She talked to him, she played with him, she admired him, and she raised him in her eyes from a slave to a king.

Those crowned with beauty are always kings,
Even if they are in rags or sold as slaves.

A true king is always a king, with or without a throne.

The friends and relations of Zuleikha began to tell tales about her having fallen in love with Yusuf. And, as it is natural for people to take interest in the faults of others, it eventually put Zuleikha in a difficult position.

She invited all her relations and friends and put into the hands of each of them a lemon and a knife. She told them all to cut the lemons when she should tell them, and then called Yusuf. When he came she told them to cut the lemons, but the eyes of every one among them were so attracted by the appearance of Yusuf that many instead of cutting the lemon cut their fingers, thereby stamping on their fingers also the love of Yusuf.

Beauty takes away from the lover the consciousness of self.

Zuleikha, so entirely won by Yusuf, forgot in the love of him what is right and what is wrong.

Reason falls when love rises.

They became more intimate every day, until a spell of passion came and separated them. When the shadow of passion fell upon the soul of Yusuf, Zuleikha happened to think of covering the face of the idol which was in her room. This astonished Yusuf and made him ask her, "What dost thou?"

She said, "I cover the face of my god that seeth us with his eyes full of wrath."

This startled Yusuf. He saw the vision of his father pointing his finger towards heaven. Yusuf said, "Stay, O Zuleikha, of what hast thou put me in mind! The eyes of thy god can be covered with a piece of cloth, but the eyes of my God cannot be covered. He seeth me wherever I am."

He is man who remembers God in anger and fears God in passion.

Zuleikha, blinded by the overwhelming darkness of passion, would not desist, and when he still refused, her passion turned into wrath. She hated him and cursed him and reminded him of his low position as a slave.

On this he began to leave the room. She caught him by the nape of the neck, and thus Yusuf's garment was torn. The chief happened to enter the room during this. He was amazed at this sight, which neither Zuleikha nor Yusuf could hide.

Before he asked her anything she complained to him, in order to hide her evident fault, that Yusuf had made an attempt to lay hands upon her. This naturally enraged the chief, and he at once gave orders that Yusuf should be taken to prison for life.

The righteous have more trials in life than the unrighteous.

Prison was a delight to the truthful Yusuf, who had kept his torch alight through the darkness of passion while walking in the path of love.

It was not long before the spell upon Zuleikha faded, and then came a settled melancholy. There was no end to her sorrow and repentance.

Love dies in passion, and is again born of passion.

Years passed, and the pain of Zuleikha's heart consumed her flesh and blood. She wasted away. On one side was the love of Yusuf; on the other side the constant trouble that her guilty conscience caused her and the idea that her own beloved had been thrown into prison on her account, which almost took her life away.

Time, which changes all things, changed the conditions of Yusuf's life. Though he was in prison he had never blamed Zuleikha, by reason of her love. He became every day more deeply immersed in the thought of her, and yet remained firm in his principle, which is the sign of the godly.

He was loved and liked by those in the prison, and he interpreted their dreams whenever they asked him. Yusuf's presence made the prison heaven for the prisoners. But Zuleikha, after the death of her husband, fell into still greater misery.

After many years it happened that Pharaoh dreamed a dream which greatly startled and alarmed him. Among all the soothsayers and magicians in the land there was none who could interpret his dream.

Then he was told by his servants of Yusuf and his wonderful gift of interpreting dreams. He sent for Yusuf, who after having been told Pharaoh's dream gave the interpretation of it. By his wise counsel he greatly relieved the king in his cares. Pharaoh made him chief over all his treasures, and bestowed on him honor and power that raised him in the eyes of the world.

Verily the truth at last is victorious.

Then his brothers came to Yusuf, and afterwards his father Jacob, who was released from the years of pain that he had suffered through his love of Yusuf.

The reward of love never fails the lover.

Once Yusuf, riding with his retinue, happened to pass by the place where Zuleikha in her utter misery was spending her days. On hearing the sound of the horses' hoofs, many people ran to see the company passing, and all called out, "It is Yusuf, Yusuf!"

On hearing this, Zuleikha desired to look at him once again. When Yusuf saw her he did not recognize her, but he halted, seeing that some woman wished to speak to him. He was moved to see a person in such misery, and asked her, "What desireth thou of me?"

She said, "Zuleikha has still the same desire, O Yusuf, and it will continue here and in the hereafter. I have desired thee, and thee alone I will desire."

Yusuf became convinced of her constant love, and was moved by her state of misery. He kissed her on the forehead, and took her in his arms and prayed to God. The prayer of the prophet and the appeal of long-continued love attracted the blessing of God, and Zuleikha regained her youth and beauty. Yusuf said to Zuleikha, "From this day thou becomest my beloved queen." They were then married and lived in happiness.

Verily God hearkens attentively to the cry of every wretched heart.

Solomon

There is a story told of Solomon, that he had a vision that God revealed Himself to him and said, "Ask what I shall give thee."

Solomon said, "Give me an understanding heart, wisdom, and knowledge."

And God said to him, "Because thou hast asked this thing and hast not asked long life for thyself, neither hast thou asked riches for thyself, but hast asked for thyself understanding, behold! I have done according to thy word. I have given thee a wise and an understanding heart. And I have also given thee that which thou hast not asked, both riches and honor, and I will lengthen thy days."

Timurlenk

There is a story of Timurlenk, the great Moghul emperor, a man whom destiny had intended to be great. Yet he was not awakened to that greatness.

One day, tired of the strife of daily life and overwhelmed by his worldly duties, he was lying on the ground in a forest waiting for death to come and take him.

A dervish passed by and saw him asleep, and recognized in him the man that destiny had intended to become a great personality. The dervish struck him with his stick and Timurlenk woke up and asked, "Why have you come to trouble me here? I have left the world and have come to the forest. Why do you come to trouble me?"

The dervish said, "What gain is there in the forest? You have the whole world before you. It is there that you will find what you have to accomplish, if only you realize the power that is within you."

He said, "No, I am too disappointed, too passionate for any good to come to me. The world has wounded me; I am sore, my heart is broken. I will no longer stay in this world."

The dervish said, "What is the use of having come to this earth if you have not accomplished something, if you have not experienced something? If you are not happy, you do not know how to live!"

Timurlenk said to the dervish, "Do you think that I shall ever accomplish anything?"

The dervish answered, "That is why I have come to awaken you. Wake up and pursue your duty with courage. You will be successful; there is no doubt about it."

This impression awakened in Timurlenk the spirit with which he had come into the world. And with every step that he took forward, he saw that conditions changed and all the influences and forces that he needed for success came to him as if life, which before had closed its doors, now opened all to him. And he reached the state where he became the famous Timurlenk of history.

Surdas

Surdas, a very great musician and poet of India, was deeply in love with a singer and took delight in seeing her. His fondness so increased that he could not live a single day without her.

Once there was a heavy rainfall which continued for weeks, and the country towns were all flooded. There was no means of getting about. The roads were impassable, but nothing would prevent Surdas from seeing his beloved at the promised time. He set out through the heavy rain, but on the way there was a river which was in flood and unfordable. There was no boat in sight. Surdas therefore jumped into the river and tried to swim.

The rough waves of the river buffeted him, raised him up and threw him down as if from mountains to the abyss. Fortunately he was thrown against a corpse, of which (taking it to be a log of wood) he seized hold. He clung to it and arrived in the end, after a great struggle, at the cottage of his beloved.

He found the doors locked. It was late at night and any

noise would have roused the whole neighborhood. Therefore he tried to climb up the house and enter through the upper window. He took hold of a cobra, which seemed like a rope hanging, thinking that it had perhaps been put there on purpose for him by his beloved.

When she saw him she was amazed. She could not understand how he had managed to come, and the impression that his love made on her was greater than ever. She was as if inspired by his love. He was raised in her ideal from a man to an angel, especially when she discovered that he had taken a corpse for a log of wood and a cobra, the enemy of man, for a rope of safety. She saw how death is slain by the lover.

She said to him, "O man, thy love is higher than the average man's love. If only it could be for God, the supreme deity, how great a bliss it would be! Rise, then, above the love of form and matter, and direct thy love to the spirit of God."

He took her advice like a simple child, and left her with heavy heart. From that time onward he wandered in the forests of India. For many years he roamed in the forests, repeating the name of the Divine Beloved and seeking refuge in His arms. He visited the sacred places, the places of pilgrimage, and by chance reached the bank of a holy river where the women of the city came every morning at sunrise to fill their pitchers with the sacred water.

Surdas, sitting there in the thought of God, was struck by the beauty and charm of one among them. His heart, being a torch, did not take long to light. He followed this woman. When she entered her house she told her husband, "Some sage saw me at the river and has followed me to the house, and he is still standing outside."

The thoughtful husband went out immediately, and saw this man with the face of a sage and spiritual dignity shed around him. He said, "O Maharaj, what has made thee tarry here? Is there anything that I can do for thee?"

Surdas said, "Who was the woman who entered this house?"

He said, "She is my wife, and she and I are both at the service of sages."

Surdas said, "Pray ask her to come, O blessed one, that I may see her once more." And when she came out he looked at her once and said, "O Mother, pray bring me two pins." And when she brought them to him he bowed to her charm and beauty once more and thrust the pins into his eyes, saying, "O my eyes, ye will nevermore see and be tempted by earthly beauty and cast me down from heaven to earth."

Then he was blind for the rest of his life.

His songs of the divine ideal are still alive and are sung by the God-loving people in India. And if any Hindu is blind, people call him Surdas, which he takes as a term of honor and respect.

Usman Haruni

There is a story about a great Sufi in India, whose name was Usman Haruni. He was a murshid to whom came thousands of disciples, among them many of the most learned and philosophical people of the time. He taught them the deepest truths of mysticism, and most of all to worship the nameless and formless God.

But there came a time when he said to them, "So far I have worshipped according to tradition, but now I feel that I must go and prostrate myself before the image of the goddess Kali in all humility."

His pupils were aghast. That he, whose conception of God had been so lofty, should go and bow before the hideous image of Kali, to worship whom was to break the law of their religion, was beyond anything they could conceive, and caused them to fear that their master had lost his reason. Some even thought that he was treading the downward path.

So when the teacher went to the temple of Kali, only one of his pupils went with him, a youth whose devotion to his master was very great. As they went, the teacher said to this disciple,

"You should go back. They are many, and are surely in the right; I am perhaps in the wrong."

But the young man still followed. When the temple was reached, the teacher was so greatly moved by the thoughts that the image of the goddess suggested to him that he prostrated himself in humility. And the disciple, standing by, looked on with sympathy at the thought of how many followers his master had had, and of how in one moment all had turned from him.

When the teacher arose he said, "Do you still follow me?" And when the disciple said that he did, the holy man asked him further, "But perhaps you do not understand why you follow me?"

Then the youth said, "You have taught me the first lesson of the spiritual path: that none exists save God. How then can I exclude this image of Kali if you choose to bow and prostrate yourself before it?"

Sin and Virtue

A story is told that Moses was going to Mount Sinai. On his way he met a very pious person, who said to him, "Moses, speak to God of me. All my life I have been pious, I have been virtuous, I have prayed to God; and I have had nothing but troubles and misfortunes."

A little later Moses met a man sitting in the street with a bottle of liquor. He called out, "Moses! Where are you going?"

Moses said, "To Mount Sinai."

The man called out, "To Mount Sinai? Then speak to God of me," for he was drunk.

Moses went to Mount Sinai and he told God of the pious person whom he had met. God said, "For him there is a place in the heavens."

Then he told God of the drunken man whom he had met. God said, "He shall be sent to the worst possible place in hell."

Moses went away and first he met the drunken man. He told him, "God says you shall be sent to the worst possible place in hell.'' The man said, ''God spoke of me?'' And he was so overjoyed that he could not contain himself, but began to dance, just as a poor man might be overjoyed if he heard that a king had spoken of him, even if the king had said nothing good of him. Then he said, ''How happy should I be that He, the Creator and Sovereign of the universe, knows me, the great sinner.''

Then Moses told the pious person what God had said. He said, ''Why not? I have spent all my life in the worship of God and in piety, sacrificing all else in life, and therefore I am entitled to have it.''

Both the pious person and the drunkard died, and Moses was curious to know what had become of them. He went to Mount Sinai and asked God.

God said, ''The pious person is in hell, and the drunken man is in heaven.''

Moses thought, ''Does God break His word?''

God said, ''The drunkard's joy on hearing that We had spoken of him has wiped out all his sins. The pious person's virtue was worthless. Why could he not be satisfied if We made the sun shine and sent the rain?''

Honesty

There is the story of a boy who was sent to Baghdad across the desert, after his mother had sewn a few gold coins in his blanket, telling him to keep it safe and not open it till he reached the city. This was the precaution against robbers, for there were no trains or cars or caravans; it was necessary to travel alone and on foot.

When this lad came to the desert, robbers met him. Thinking he would not have much money, being only a little boy, they asked him all the same, "Have you any coins, any gold, any silver?" Having been trained to tell the truth, he answered, "Yes, I have." His conscience would never permit him to answer no.

"Where are they?" they asked.

"They are sewn in this blanket," he said.

But the very fact of his telling them won the robbers' hearts and made them act rightly themselves. They said, "We would have stolen them had you not told the truth," and they let him go free.

Anger

There is a story about a great Sufi master who lived in Arabia. During some war a certain battle was fought. Now in those days battles were hand-to-hand fights, and this man's enemy was overpowered by him and he was about to kill him.

But at this moment the enemy spat in his face. The teacher immediately let go of the man and did not kill him. The enemy was greatly surprised at this and said, "You were about to kill me; why did you not do so?"

He replied, "The reason is that you did something that was bound to rouse my anger, and if I had killed you while under the influence of anger I would have acted against my principles. Therefore, as soon as I caught myself in this fault, I became unable to carry through my first intention."

In The Mirror

Some time ago there was in Delhi a mystic or murshid whose name was Shah Alam. One day he was having a haircut. He was looking in a little looking glass, such as are used in India, while the barber was cutting his hair.

Suddenly he dashed the mirror on the ground so that it broke into pieces. His mureeds, who were with him, were astonished. The barber also was amazed, wondering what had caused him to throw down the mirrow with such violence.

Afterwards he told them what had happened. At that time one of his mureeds was travelling by sea from Arabia to India. A storm had struck the ship he was sailing in, and he was in great danger. He called upon his murshid for help, and the murshid saw his peril in the mirror and saved him.

Balance

A disciple was taught by Muhammad a practice by which he experienced ecstasy.

After some days he came bringing fruit and flowers, which he offered to the Prophet, thanking him greatly and saying, "The lesson that you taught me has been of such great value to me; it has brought me such joy. My prayers, which used to last a few minutes, now last all day."

Muhammad said, "I am glad that you liked the lesson, but please, from today, stop the practice!"

Ego Always Wants

Dervishes sometimes do humorous things. There is a story about a certain dervish sitting in the shade of a tree, who was always very kind and helpful to those who came to see him.

But one day a young man, a soldier, was passing by, and he said something to the dervish which made him cross. So they had a few words. Thereupon the soldier began to bully him and give him blows on his back and neck, without the dervish making any protest. The soldier then went on his way.

A wise man sitting nearby was thinking to himself, "What a funny thing. For this dervish is always good and kind and hospitable, so why should the soldier be so angry as to punch him and hit him all over?"

So he watched attentively and noticed the dervish saying to himself, "Is it enough, or do you want some more?"

The man wondered why the dervish said this. But the explanation is that the ego always wants feeding, and the more you feed it the more energy it has.

Two Black Marks

An Arab had lost his camel. After searching for it everywhere he heard that it was in the stable of the sheriff of Mecca.

He went to the sheriff and said, "I have been told that my she-camel, which I lost, has been sold to you and is in your stable."

The sheriff asked him, "How will you recognize your camel? Has she any particular marks?"

The Arab said, "She has two black marks upon her heart."

The sheriff was amazed to hear this, wondering how the Arab could know about his camel's heart. In order to ascertain the truth the camel was cut open. Two black marks were found upon her heart.

The sheriff asked, "How could you know that your camel had those two black marks upon her heart?"

The Arab replied, "Twice my camel was in great sorrow: twice she lost her foal. Each time she looked up and gave a deep sigh, and I knew that a black mark was left upon her heart."

The Power of Trust

There is a story of a great Sufi who in his early life was a robber.

Once there was a man travelling through the desert in a caravan, and he had a purse full of coins. He wanted to entrust them to someone because he had heard that robbers were about.

He looked around and some way off he saw a tent, and a man was sitting there, a most distinguished-looking man. So he said, "Will you please keep this purse? For I am afraid that if the robbers come they will take it."

The man said, "Give it to me, I will keep it."

When the traveller came back to the caravan, he found that robbers had come and taken all the money of his fellow-travellers, and he thanked God that he had given his purse to someone to keep.

But when he returned to the tent he saw all the robbers sitting there, and among them was this most dignified man dividing the spoils. He realized that this was the chief of the robbers and thought, "I was more foolish than all the others, for I gave my money to a thief. Who can be more foolish than that!'' And he was frightened and backed away.

But as soon as the chief saw him he called to him and said, ''Why are you going? Why did you come here?''

He said, ''I came here to get my purse back, but I found that I had given it to the very band from which I wanted to protect it.''

The chief said, ''You gave me your purse, is it not so? You entrusted it to me, and it was not stolen from you. Did you not trust me? How can you expect me to take it from you? Here is your purse, take it.''

This act of trustworthiness impressed the robbers so much that they followed the example of their chief. They gave up robbery. It moved them to the depths of their hearts to feel what trust means. And in his later days this chief accomplished great spiritual work.

This shows that by distrusting people we perhaps avoid a little loss, but the distrust that we have sown in our heart is a still greater loss.

True Faith

There is a story told of a dervish, a simple man who was initiated by a teacher. After the teacher had passed away, this man came into contact with a clairvoyant, who asked him if he had guidance on his path.

The man replied, "Yes, my master, who passed from this earth. When he was still alive I enjoyed his guidance for some time, so the only thing I would want now is just your blessing."

But the clairvoyant said, "I see by my clairvoyant power that the teacher who has passed away was not a true teacher."

When the simple man heard this he would not allow himself to be angry with the other, but he said gently, "This teacher of mine may be false, but my faith is not false, and that is sufficient."

The Magic Wand

A child said to its guardian, "I would like to have a magic wand. Where could I get it?"

The guardian said, "If you had a magic wand what would you do with it?"

The child answered, "I heard that if a person has a magic wand he has only to wave it and everything will come."

So the guardian said, "What do you wish?"

At first the child hesitated, because he felt very shy about telling his wish, but in the end he expressed his wish.

As soon as the guardian knew, he said, "You do not need a magic wand; the wish itself is a power if you can think about it."

The child said, "I always think about it."

The guardian said, "Think about it still more."

Zeb-un-nisa

In the veiling and unveiling of beauty lies every purpose of creation.

The shah of Persia, who loved the beautiful princess Zeb-un-nisa for the thoughts she disclosed in her verses, once wrote to her, "Though I bear your image in my mind, I would never permit my eyes to raise themselves to your face." At another time he wrote asking her, "What sort of love is yours that you do not unveil your beauty to me?"

She answered, referring to the tale of Majnun and Leila, who are the Romeo and Juliet of the East, "Though my heart is the heart of Majnun, yet I am of the sex of Leila. And though my sighs are deep, *hayya* (modesty) is a chain upon my feet."

The fame of her learning and beauty spread far and wide, but Zeb-un-nisa never married. A poet, a philosopher, she lived absorbed in her own meditations and studies. She never saw her lover, although for long they exchanged verses in an intellectual interchange of thoughts on life, truth, and beauty.

After many years, he wrote in passionate longing to her that if he could see her but once it would be to him a sacred vision. In answer she sent a poem that said:

The nightingale would forget his song to the rose,
If he saw Me walking in the garden.
If the Brahman saw My face,
He would forget his idol.
Whoever would find Me,
Must look in My words;
For I am hidden in My words,
As the perfume in the petals of the flowers.

Thus she replied to his desire to see a sacred vision, describing the divine veiling of the divine presence. Even in this way have all those who touched the divine life and caught sight of the divine beauty spoken of their inspirations. Remember the words of Krishna, who said, "Whenever *dharma* [religion] is threatened, then am I born."

Umar

There is a story of Umar, the well-known khalif of Arabia. Someone who wanted to harm Umar was looking for him. He heard that Umar did not live in palaces, though he was a king, but that he spent most of his time with nature. This man was very glad to think that now he would have every opportunity to accomplish his object.

He approached the place where Umar was sitting, but the nearer he came the more his attitude changed; until in the end he dropped the dagger which was in his hand and said, "I cannot harm you. Tell me what is the power in you that keeps me from accomplishing the object which I came to accomplish?" And Umar answered, "My at-one-ment with God."

Discrimination

The nawab of Rampur once expressed a desire to the chief musician of his court to learn music himself.

The master said, "I will teach you music on one condition, and that is that you do not listen to every kind of music that comes your way. When bad music is heard the ear becomes spoiled; and then you cannot discriminate between bad music and good music."

Iblis

There is a very interesting story told in the Arabic scriptures. It is that God made Iblis the chief among the angels, and then told him to bring some clay that He might make out of it an image.

The angels, under the direction of Iblis, brought the clay and made an image; then God breathed into that image, and asked the angels to bow before it.

All the angels bowed; but Iblis said, "Lord, Thou hast made me the chief of all angels, and I have brought this clay at Thy command, and made with my own hands this image which Thou commandest me to bow before."

The displeasure of God arose and fell on his neck as the sign of the outcast.

Rustam

A great king of Persia named Jamshyd had a certain wrestler named Rustam. He was the greatest of all wrestlers in the kingdom, and he became so proud of his strength and power and bravery that the king thought he would humble him in some way. But he could not find anyone who could be trained to be capable of matching Rustam: he was the only one of his kind in the whole land.

Then it happened that Rustam went to Arabia, and during his absence a son was born to him, who was given the name of Kushtam. The child's mother died soon after, and this was the opportunity the king sought. He took the child into his palace, and no one knew he was Rustam's son. In the course of time the youth became a great fighter, so strong and powerful that no one in the land could match him.

And then, after many years, Rustam returned. Jamshyd did not tell the youth that Rustam was his father; he only said that a powerful wrestler had come from Arabia, and that he must fight him.

Now it was the custom for every wrestler to wear a dagger

with which to kill a vanquished opponent if he refused to surrender. Everybody went to see the wrestling match in the arena. The king felt sure that Kushtam, the son, would conquer his father. And indeed, with great energy and strength, the young man brought Rustam down.

But Rustam, being so proud of his great power throughout his life, did not wish to surrender, so he must be killed. Kushtam unsheathed his dagger, whereupon Rustam said, "It does not matter. Someday, when my son grows up, he will vanquish you."

The youth asked, "Who is your son?"

Rustam then said, "But who are you?"

And then the secret came out that this youth was his own son. There was no end to Kushtam's sorrow. He made obeisance at his father's feet, saying, "Father, I would rather be the one to be killed than be your conqueror."

His father replied, "Do not let it grieve you, for now I am happy to know that at least I have not been vanquished by anyone but my own son, who is my own self."

Haris Chandra

One day the rishis were conversing, and they wondered whether there existed on earth one human being who was fully dependable. And the answer was, "One there is. His name is King Haris Chandra!" But they said, "King Haris Chandra! He has got all that the heart could wish. He has a prospering kingdom; his subjects adore him; he has a loving wife and a promising son. How can we know whether he is really dependable?"

So the rishis agreed to test King Haris Chandra. One of them went in the guise of a sage, saying, "King Haris Chandra, will you grant me a wish?"

And King Haris Chandra, who was at the service of the sages, said, "Yes, I will grant it."

The rishi said, "King Haris Chandra, I wish to be king over this country."

And Haris Chandra went to his wife and said, "Come with me; I am no longer king." So they went, he and his wife and their little son, on foot to the neighboring country.

When they had reached the boundary, the rishi appeared,

saying, "You have travelled so many days in my kingdom. Now pay me the tax you owe me."

Haris Chandra said, "Nothing I have with which I can pay you."

But the rishi said, "Haris Chandra, you gave me your word that I am the king of this land, so pay me the tax."

Then Haris Chandra sold his wife and his son as slaves to be able to pay the tax to the king. He himself entered into the service of the one who owned the burning ghat at Benares, and at the entrance he collected the money for his master.

While he was doing that work his little son suddenly fell ill and died. His wife came with her dead boy in her arms, that he might be cremated at the burning ghat. Haris Chandra put forward his hand to receive her due. But what has a poor slave to offer? She had nothing to give. Then Haris Chandra kept faithful to his master, and refused her entry.

At that moment the rishi put an end to the test. He restored the dead prince to life, and made Haris Chandra again king over his country.

A Shah of Persia

A shah of Persia used to sit up at night for his vigils and prayers. And a friend who was visiting him wondered at his long meditations after the whole day's work. "It is too much," he said, "you do not need so much meditation."

"Do not say so," was the answer. "You do not know. For at night I pursue God, and during the day God follows me."

Hakim

In the East there is a well-known story about a young man called Hakim and a princess who was renowned for her beauty. There were many who loved her and wanted to marry her, but she had made a condition: that the one who brought her a certain pearl which she longed to possess would be accepted. One lover of this princess loved her perhaps more than anybody else, but he could not find a way of getting the pearl.

Now Hakim's task in life was to roam about from country to country doing what he could for those who needed his services. He met this lover, who was very unhappy; and Hakim consoled him and said, "Continue in your pursuit of love even if it be difficult, and remember that I shall go on until I have brought rest to your heart by finding for you the pearl you are looking for."

Hakim went in pursuit of the pearl, and the story goes on to tell what difficulties he had in obtaining it. At last he got it and brought it to the palace, and then the princess was so impressed by Hakim that she declared that she wanted him as her husband. But Hakim told her of the promise he had made to his friend, who was her real lover. He himself was the lover of those in need.

The Servant

The disciples of Khwaja Nizam ad-din Wali, a great saint of Delhi, were once sitting waiting for him to come and speak upon a very abstruse and difficult matter; when to their astonishment they saw his servant come into the room and sit down on the murshid's seat.

Nizam ad-din then came in, made a very deep bow to the servant, and took his seat before him. The servant began to speak, and spoke for some time, explaining some very subtle and deep questions.

Then a change came over his face. He looked around and ran from the room in great confusion.

Afterwards Nizam ad-din told his disciples that he had asked his murshid for the answer to some very difficult question. The subject was so complex that the murshid needed a human form in order to explain it exactly, and that was why he had spoken through the servant.

Shigrakavi

There is an amusing story about two great Hindustani poets whose habit it was to speak in poetry. Poets who were able to do this were called *shigrakavi*.

One of them was very thin, while the other was very stout. One came to the village where the other poet was living. The fat one asked the thin one, in verse, if he was well. And the other answered, "The temple which is meant for God to live in does not need flesh; one must be thankful that there are bones!" And he added, "But you look quite well."

Whereupon the stout poet answered, "When I had not yet found my beloved I also was thin, but the moment my beloved came to me I became fat."

The Fearless One

A young man one day said to his friends, "You can send me to any place that is haunted. I can stand it, for I do not believe in such things."

One friend asked him, "Do you think you can stay all night in the graveyard?" He said yes.

So all night long he stayed there without any fear. Nothing appeared. But just before sunrise, when he got up after waiting all night for the ghost and started to leave the graveyard, his long cloak was caught by some thorns on the ground and he felt a pull. That shock made him faint, and he almost died.

Laws

It was the custom in a country where the people lived by agriculture that each man should receive as his portion a certain plot of land. Some availed themselves of the privilege, and others disregarded their inheritance.

Now one man, a good husbandman, saw a field lying untouched and unclaimed, and he passionately desired it. He knew that by his labor it could become a fair and beautiful place. And going to the ruler of his country, he demanded of him this field he had found lying waste and unclaimed.

The ruler replied, "You are a good husbandman; you have in no wise neglected that which you have; and for myself, I feel grieved that this goodly field that you have seen should lie overlooked. For it is my desire that my land should be a happy and rich country, and that every part of it should be filled with prosperity.

"But if I should grant to you this portion, what restraint could I have over dishonest and neglectful husbandmen? For it is rare to find a man such as yourself. For the most part the husbandmen are slothful and thriftless, thieving and dishonest, scarcely worthy to keep that possession and that liberty which they already have, but ready at all times to snatch at what is not theirs by right."

"But," said the good husbandman to the ruler, "if a portion of land remains unclaimed, weeds will grow and all manner of harmful things may breed there. So there is a double loss to your country, for these harmful things spread to other enclosed and cultivated places, and the seeds of the weeds are blown everywhere by the wind."

"This I know well," said the ruler of the country, "but it is my duty to make my laws having regard to the worst of my subjects."

Wise Love

There is a story told of Sa'adi, that chivalrous and most ideal of poets. He loved a girl very dearly. He admired and valued her more than all else in his life, so that there was nothing that he would not do for her sake.

Coming to see her one day he found her—though he could scarcely believe his eyes—in the arms of another. Going away quietly, he took his stand at the gateway of her house.

When the other man saw Sa'adi standing there he thought, "Surely now, filled with jealousy, he is waiting to kill me."

But Sa'adi, as he saw him approach, called, "Friend, be at peace. I am waiting to give you a word of good advice: that as I have seen and gone away quietly, so do you, if you should see her in the arms of another. For that is the way in which the wise love."

Meditation

A young man asked his mother, who was a peasant woman living in a village, "What is the best occupation, Mother?"

And the mother said, "I do not know, Son, except that those who search after the highest in life go in search of God."

"Then where must I go, Mother?" he asked.

She answered, "I do not know whether it is practical or not, but they say in the solitude, in the forest."

So he went there for a long time and lived a life of patience and solitude. And once or twice in between he came to see his mother. Sometimes his patience was exhausted, his heart broken. Sometimes he was disappointed in not finding God. And each time the mother sent him back with stronger advice. At the third visit she said, "Now I think you are ready to go to a teacher."

So he went to see a teacher. And there were many pupils learning under that teacher. Every pupil had a little room to himself for meditation, and this pupil also was told to go into a certain room to meditate.

The teacher asked, "Is there anything you love in the world?"

This young man, having been away from home since childhood, not having seen anything of the world, could think of no one he knew, except of the little cow that was in his house.

He said, "I love the cow in our house."

The teacher said, "Then think of the cow in your meditation."

All the other pupils came and went, and sat in their rooms for fifteen minutes for a little meditation. Then they got tired and went away. But this young man remained sitting there from the time the teacher had told him to.

After some time the teacher asked, "Where is he?"

The other pupils answered, "We don't know. He must be in his room."

They went to look for him. The door was closed and there was no answer. The teacher went himself and opened the door, and there he saw the pupil sitting in meditation, fully absorbed in it. And when the teacher called him by name, he answered in the sound of the cow. The teacher said, "Come out."

He answered, "My horns are too large to pass through the door."

Then the teacher said to his pupils, "Look, this is the living example of meditation. You are meditating on God and you do not know where God is, but he is meditating on the cow and he has become the cow; he has lost his identity. He has identified himself with the object on which he meditates."

The Hereafter

A pessimist came to Hazrat Ali and said, "Is there really a hereafter for which you are preparing us by telling us to refrain from things that we desire and to live a life of goodness and piety? What if there is no such thing as a hereafter?"

Ali answered, "If there is no such thing as a hereafter, I shall be in the same situation as you are; but if there is a hereafter, then I shall be the gainer, and you will be the loser!"

Leila and Majnun

The story of Leila and Majnun has been told in the East for thousands of years, and has always exerted a great fascination. For it is not only a love story, but a lesson in love; not love as it is generally understood by man, but the love that rises above the earth and heavens.

A lad called Majnun from childhood had shown love in his nature, revealing to the eye of the seers the tragedy of his life.

When Majnun was at school he became fond of Leila. In time the spark grew into a flame, and Majnun did not feel at rest if Leila was a little late in coming; with his book in his hand, he fixed his eyes on the entrance, which amused the scoffers and disturbed everybody there.

The flame in time rose into a blaze, and then Leila's heart became kindled by Majnun's love. Each looked at the other; she did not see anyone in the class but Majnun, nor did he see anyone save Leila.

In reading from a book Majnun would read the name of Leila; in writing dictation Leila would cover her slate with the name of Majnun.

All else disappears when the thought of the beloved
occupies the mind of the lover.

Everyone in the school whispered to each other, pointing them out. The teachers were worried and wrote to the parents of both that their children were crazy and intensely fond of one another, and that there seemed no way to divert their attention from their love affair, which had stopped every possibility of their progress in study.

Leila's parents removed her at once, and kept a careful watch over her. In this way they took her away from Majnun; but who could take Majnun away from her heart? She had no thought but of Majnun.

Without her, Majnun, in his heart's unrest and grief, kept the whole school in a turmoil, until his parents were compelled to take him home, as there seemed to be nothing left for him in the school.

Majnun's parents called physicians, soothsayers, healers, magicians, and poured money at their feet, asking them for some remedy to take away from the heart of Majnun the thought of Leila. But how could it be done?

Even Luqman, the great physician of the ancients,
had no cure for the lovesick.

No one has ever healed a patient of love. Friends came, relations came, well-wishers came, wise counselors came; and all tried their best to efface from his mind the thought of Leila. But all was in vain.

Someone said to him, "O Majnun, why do you sorrow at the separation from Leila? She is not beautiful. I can show you a thousand fairer and more charming maidens, and can let you choose your mate from among them." Majnun answered, "Oh, to see the beauty of Leila, the eyes of Majnun are needed."

When no remedy had been left untried, the parents of Majnun resolved to seek the refuge of the Ka'bah as their last resort.

They took Majnun on the pilgrimage to Mecca. When they drew near to the Ka'bah, a great crowd gathered to see them. The parents, each in turn, went and prayed to God, saying, "O Lord, Thou art most merciful and compassionate. Grant Thy favor to our only son, that the heart of Majnun may be released from the pain of the love of Leila."

Everybody there listened to this intently, and wonderingly awaited what Majnun had to say. Majnun was told by his parents, "Child, go and pray that the love of Leila may be taken away from your heart."

Majnun replied, "Shall I meet my Leila if I pray?"

They, with the greatest disappointment, said, "Pray, Child, whatever you like to pray."

He went, and said, "I want my Leila," and everybody present said, "Amen."

The world echoes to the lover's call.

When the parents had sought in every way to cure Majnun of his craze for Leila, in the end they thought the best way was to approach the parents of Leila, for this was the last hope of saving Majnun's life. They sent a message to Leila's parents, who were of another faith, saying, "We have done all we can to take away from Majnun the thought of Leila, but so far we have not succeeded, nor is there any hope of success left to us except one. That is your consent to their marriage.''

In answer, they said, ''Although it exposes us to the scorn of our people, still Leila seems never to forget the thought of Majnun for one single moment; and since we have taken her away from school she pines away every day. Therefore, we should not mind giving Leila in marriage to Majnun, if only we were convinced that he is sane.''

On hearing this the parents of Majnun were much pleased, and advised Majnun to behave sensibly, so that Leila's parents might have no cause to suspect him of being out of his mind.

Majnun agreed to do everything his parents desired, if he could only meet his Leila. They went, according to the custom of the East, in procession to the house of the bride, where a special seat was made for the bridegroom, who was covered with garlands of flowers.

But, as they say in the East, the gods are against lovers. So destiny did not grant these perfect lovers the happiness of being together.

The dog that used to accompany Leila to school happened to come into the room where they were sitting. As soon as Majnun's eyes fell on this dog his emotion broke out. He could not sit in the high seat and look at the dog. He ran to the dog and kissed its paws and put all the garlands of flowers on the neck of the dog. There was no sign of reverence or worship that Majnun did not show to this dog.

The dust of the beloved's dwelling is the earth of
Ka'bah to the lover.

This conduct plainly proved him insane. As love's language is gibberish to the loveless, so the action of Majnun was held by those present to be mere folly. They were all greatly disappointed, and Majnun was taken back home. And Leila's parents refused their consent to the marriage.

This utter disappointment made Majnun's parents altogether hopeless, and they no longer kept watch over him, seeing that life and death to him were both the same. This gave Majnun freedom to wander about the town in search of Leila, enquiring of everyone he met about her.

By chance he met a letter carrier who was carrying mail on the back of a camel; and when Majnun asked this man Leila's whereabouts, he said, "Her parents have left this country and have gone to live a hundred miles from here."

Majnun begged him to give his message to Leila. He said, "With pleasure." But when Majnun began to tell him the message, the telling continued for a long, long time.

The message of love has no end.

The letter carrier was partly amused, and partly he sympathized with his earnestness. Although Majnun, walking with his camel, was company for him on his long journey, still, out of pity, he said, "Now you have walked ten miles giving me your message. How long will it take me to deliver it to Leila? Now go your way, I will see to it."

Then Majnun turned back, but he had not gone a hundred yards before he returned to say, "O kind friend, I have forgotten to tell you a few things that you might tell my Leila."

When he continued his message it carried him another ten

miles on the way. The carrier said, "For mercy's sake, go back. You have walked a long way. How shall I be able to remember all the message you have given me? Still I will do my best. Now go back, you are far from home."

Majnun again went back a few yards, and again remembered something to tell the message bearer and went after him. In this way the whole journey was accomplished, and he himself arrived at the place to which he was sending the message.

The letter carrier was astonished at this earnest love, and said to him, "You have already arrived in the land where your Leila lives. Now stay in this ruined mosque. This is outside the town; if you go with me into the town they will torment you before you can reach Leila. The best thing is for you to rest here now, as you have walked so very far, and I will convey your message to Leila as soon as I can reach her."

Love's intoxication sees no time nor space.

Majnun listened to his advice and stayed there, and felt inclined to rest, but the idea that he was in the town where Leila dwelt made him wonder in which direction he should stretch out his legs.

He thought of the north, south, east, and west, and thought to himself, "If Leila were on this side it would be insolent on my part to stretch out my feet towards her. The best thing, then, would be to hang my feet by a rope from above, for surely she will not be there."

The lover's Ka'bah is the dwelling-place of the beloved.

He was thirsty, and could find no water except some rainwater that had collected in a disused tank.

When the letter carrier entered the house of Leila's parents, he saw Leila and said to her, "I had to make a great effort to speak with you. Your lover, Majnun, who is a lover without compare in all the world, gave me a message for you, and he continued to speak with me throughout the journey and has walked as far as this town with the camel."

She said, "For heaven's sake! Poor Majnun! I wonder what will become of him." She asked her old nurse, "What becomes of a person who has walked a hundred miles without a break?"

The nurse said rashly, "Such a person must die."

Leila said, "Is there any remedy?"

She said, "He must drink some rainwater collected for a year past, and from that water a snake must drink, and then his feet must be tied and he must be hung up in the air with his head down for a very long time; that might save his life."

Leila said, "Oh, but how difficult it is to obtain!"

God, who Himself is love, was the guide of Majnun; therefore, everything came to Majnun as was best for him.

Verily love is the healer of its own wounds.

The next morning Leila put her food aside, and sent it secretly by a maid whom she took into her confidence, with a message to tell Majnun that she longed to see him as much as he to see her, the difference being only of chains; as soon as she had an opportunity, she said, she would come at once.

The maid went to the ruined mosque, and saw two people

sitting there, one who seemed self-absorbed, unaware of his surroundings, and the other a fat, robust man. She thought that Leila could not possibly love a person like this dreamy one whom she herself would not have cared to love.

But in order to make sure, she asked which of them was named Majnun. The mind of Majnun was deeply sunk in his thought and far away from her words. But the other man, who was out of work, was rather glad to see the dinner basket in her hand, and said, "For whom are you looking?"

She said, "I am asked to give this to Majnun. Are you Majnun?"

He readily stretched out his hands to take the basket, and said, "I am the one for whom you have brought it." He spoke a word or two with her in jest, and she was delighted.

On the maid's return Leila asked, "Did you give it to him?"

She said, "Yes, I did."

Leila then sent to Majnun every day the larger part of her meals, which was received every day by this man, who was very glad to have it while out of work.

Leila one day asked her maid, "You never tell me what he says and how he eats."

She said, "He says that he sends very many thanks to you and he appreciates it very much, and he is a pleasant-spoken man. You must not worry for one moment. He is getting fatter every day."

Leila said, "But my Majnun has never been fat, and has never had a tendency to become fat; and he is too deep in his thought to say pleasant things to anyone. He is too sad to speak."

Leila at once suspected that the dinner might have been handed to the wrong person. She said, "Is anybody else there?"

The maid said, "Yes, there is another person sitting there also, but he seems to be beside himself. He never notices who comes or who goes, nor does he hear a word said by anybody there. He cannot possibly be the man that you love."

Leila said, "I think he must be the man. Alas, if you have all this time given the food to the wrong person! Well, to make sure, today take on the plate a knife instead of food, and say to that one to whom you gave the food, "For Leila a few drops of your blood are needed, to cure her of an illness."

When the maid next went to the mosque the man as usual came most eagerly to take his meal, and seeing the knife was surprised.

The maid told him that a few drops of his blood were needed to cure Leila. He said, "No, certainly I am not Majnun. There is Majnun. Ask him for it."

The maid foolishly went to him and said to him aloud, "Leila wants a few drops of your blood to cure her."

Majnun most readily took the knife in his hand and said, "How fortunate am I that my blood may be of some use to my Leila. This is nothing. Even if my life were to become a sacrifice for her cure, I would consider myself most fortunate to give it."

Whatever the lover does for the beloved, it can never be too much. He gashed his arm in several places, but the starvation of months had left no blood, nothing but skin and bone.

When a great many places had been cut hardly one drop of blood came out. He said, "That is what is left. You may take that."

Love means pain, but the lover alone is above all pain. .

Majnun's coming to the town soon became known, and when Leila's parents knew of it they thought, "Surely Leila will go out of her mind if she ever sees Majnun." Therefore they resolved to leave the town for some time, thinking that Majnun would make his way home when he found that Leila was not there. Before leaving the place Leila sent a message to Majnun to say, "We are leaving this town for a while, and I am most unhappy that I have not been able to meet you. The only chance of our meeting is that we should meet on the way, if you will go on before and wait for me in the Sahara."

Majnun started most happily to go to the Sahara, with great hope of once more seeing his Leila. When the caravan arrived in the desert and halted there for a while, the mind of Leila's parents became a little relieved, and they saw Leila also a little happier for the change, as they thought, not knowing the true reason.

Leila went for a walk in the Sahara with her maid, and suddenly came upon Majnun, whose eyes had been fixed for a long, long time on the way by which she was to come.

She came and said, "Majnun, I am here."

There remained no power in the tongue of Majnun to express his joy. He held her hands and pressed them to his breast, and said, "Leila, you will not leave me anymore?"

She said, "Majnun, I have been able to come for one

moment. If I stay any longer my people will seek for me and your life will not be safe."

Majnun said, "I do not care for life. You are my life. Oh stay! Do not leave me anymore."

Leila said, "Majnun, be sensible and believe me. I will surely come back."

Majnun let go her hands and said, "Surely I believe you."

So Leila left Majnun, with heavy heart; and Majnun, who had so long lived on his own flesh and blood, could no more stand erect, but fell backward against the trunk of a tree, which propped him up. And there he remained, living only on hope.

Years passed and the half-dead body of Majnun was exposed to all things, cold and heat and rain, frost and storm. The hands that were holding the branches became branches themselves; his body became a part of the tree.

Leila was as unhappy as before on her travels, and the parents lost hope of her life. She was living only in one hope, that she might once fulfill her promise given to Majnun at the moment of parting, saying, "I will come back." She wondered if he were alive or dead, or had gone away or whether the animals in the Sahara had carried him off.

When they returned, their caravan halted in the same place, and Leila's heart became full of joy and sorrow, of cheerfulness and gloom, of hope and fear. As she was looking for the place where she had left Majnun she met a woodcutter, who said to her, "Oh, don't go that way. There is some ghost there."

Leila said, "What is it like?"

He said, "It is a tree and at the same time man. As I struck a branch of this tree with my hatchet I heard him say in a deep sigh, 'O Leila.'"

Hearing this moved Leila beyond description. She said she would go, and drawing near the tree she saw Majnun turned almost into the tree. Flesh and blood had already wasted, and the skin and bone that remained, by contact with the tree, had become like its branches. Leila called him aloud, "Majnun!"

He answered, "Leila!"

She said, "I am here as I promised, O Majnun."

He answered, "I am Leila."

She said, "Majnun, come to your senses. I am Leila. Look at me."

Majnun said, "Are you Leila? Then I am not," and he was dead."

Leila, seeing this perfection in love, could not live a single moment more. She at the same time cried the name of Majnun and fell down and died.

The beloved is all in all, the lover only veils him.
The beloved is all that lives, the lover a dead thing.

Puran Bhagat

There is a story in the East of Puran Bhagat, who was once living in exile in the forest. After a long time, during which he had developed true love in his thought and feeling and spirit, he returned to his country.

The first thing he wished to do was to sit in his garden, which had gone to ruin during his absence. He went down to it in the guise of a sage, and began to water it with his little water bowl.

The garden at once began to flourish, and in a short time it became such a miracle of beauty that everyone in the city began to talk about it and say, "This must be some spiritual man, since the garden begins to grow and flourish."

The touch of the saints and sages and prophets makes things grow.

The Fire of Love

A mureed had been a long time in the service of a spiritual guide, but he could make no progress and was not inspired.

He went to the teacher and said, "I have seen very many mureeds being inspired, but it is my misfortune that I cannot advance at all, and now I must give up hope and leave you."

The teacher advised him to spend the last days of his stay in a house near the khanaqah. Every day he sent him very good food and told him to cease the spiritual practices and to lead a comfortable and restful life.

On the last day he sent the mureed a basket of fruit, brought by a fair damsel. She set the tray down and immediately went away, though he wished to detain her.

Her beauty and charm were so great, and he was now so much disposed to admire and was so much won by them, that he could think of nothing else. Every hour and every minute he longed only to see her again. His longing increased every moment. He forgot to eat; he was full of tears and sighs, finding his heart now warmed and melted by the fire of love.

After some time, when the teacher visited the disciple, with one glance he inspired him.

Even steel can be molded if it be heated in the fire.

And so it is with the heart which is melted by the fire of love.

The Tree That Bears All Fruit

There is an old Hindu belief, found in the ancient myths of India, that there is a tree which they call Kamana Kalpa Vraksha, a tree that bears all fruits that one can imagine. If a person is under that tree he has but to wish for what he would like, and in the same moment all fruits, all flowers, everything he can imagine he will find brought forth by the tree as its fruits. He has but to wish and it will fall into his hands. If it is within one's reach one has to raise one's hand to pluck the flower or fruit of that tree; if it is beyond one's reach one has only to wish and the branch will reach one's hand, that one may pick it without any effort.

And there is a story about that tree, that a wanderer, while journeying in deserts, by chance happened to sleep under it. And when, after a good sleep, he opened his eyes and looked up at the tree, he thought, "I suppose it must be a pear tree." No sooner had he thought that than two good ripe pears dropped near him. While lying there he picked them up.

"Oh," he said, "what a wonderful tree! If it were a grape

tree, what a splendid thing it would be!" As soon as he said it, the tree seemed full of grapes; and before he raised his hands the branches bent low and without any effort he was able to pick the grapes.

But then he thought, "What a wonderful tree!" He wondered if the tree would yield some roses. And no sooner had he given a thought to it than the whole tree seemed to blossom into roses. This man became so surprised, so amazed and perplexed at this magical tree, that he wondered if it was true or if it was only a dream. As soon as he thought of a dream and looked at the tree, the tree vanished in a moment.

Tawajjeh

There was once a conference of religions in Calcutta, and representatives of all mystical schools were invited to this congress. Shankaracharya was the leading representative of Brahmanism present. After a most impressive lecture Shankaracharya wished to sit in silence, but there was a desire on the part of the audience that some of their questions might be answered. Shankaracharya looked here and there among his disciples, and asked one of them to answer the questions.

Which disciple was this? It was someone who was not even known to Shankaracharya's pupils, for he was mostly occupied in looking after the sage's dinner or dusting his room and keeping it in order. So the people who were known to be something were not asked. This man was asked; they did not even know that he existed.

He had never done a thing like that in his whole life; it was only because he was asked that he stood up without thinking whether he would be able to give the answer or not. But the answer he gave to every question was as if it was given by Shankaracharya himself. The pupils of Shankaracharya were filled with admiration and bewildered at the same time, not having seen this man among them.

It is this which is recognized by Sufis as *tawajjeh*, reflection. It was not that pupil, it was the teacher himself who was speaking there.

Part Two

Spirits I

I had my first experience of spirits when when a boy. Once I awoke in the middle of the night feeling a wish to look out of the window into our courtyard at the beautiful moonlight shining there. I went to the window, and looking out I saw some way off a man of saintly appearance, clothed in a long white robe, with long snow-white hair and beard. I saw him as plainly as in full daylight.

I was amazed at the sight of him, wondering how it had been possible for him to enter our courtyard, all the doors being locked. But for his saintly appearance I might have supposed him to be a thief, but the nearer he came the taller he grew. At each step his height increased, until I could no longer see his head. As he came forward his figure became a mist, until at last he was like a shadow, and in a moment he vanished from my sight. My hair stood on end and I was completely overcome by bewilderment.

The next morning, when I told my family what I had seen, they tried to make nothing of it in order to keep me from superstitious beliefs. But others told me that they too had often seen this phantom appearing in the quarter.

This taught me that spirits are attached to those places in which they are interested, just as we are, and they are constantly drawn to the places of their interest. Their form is not solid but ethereal, and can expand. This phantom which I saw was that of a pir who lived in the well in our courtyard.

A few years after these first experiences I was trying to forget and disbelieve this impression, fearing that it might lead me towards superstition. But once, happening to arrive at our country cottage in the middle of the night, I found on our land a huge person at a distance of three yards from me. He made a sign that he wished to wrestle with me in the way Indians do, giving a challenge by slapping the thighs and crossing and slapping the arms.

I did not for one moment take him to be a man; I at once thought that he was a spirit. At first I was terrified, comparing my size and strength with this gigantic spirit. But I had heard that spirits swallow the fearful, so although I did not know the art of wrestling, I determined to fight with him; and I advanced, quite prepared to give him a blow. At each step that I took forward, he drew back, which naturally gave me courage to close in upon him. He retreated until he was against the wall. I was glad that now I had got him, and approaching, I struck him a strong blow; which, instead of hurting the spirit, knocked my hand against the wall. The spirit disappeared.

The reason why the spirit appears and yet has no solid form is that it exists in a vaporous state, and the image seen in this vaporous form is nothing but the impression of its former body when on earth.

Spirits II

Among very many different experiences, I cannot forget one which made a great impression upon my mind. I had purposely rented a haunted house in James Street, Sekunderabad, although my friends advised me not to. In order to experience any manifestations there I slept there alone, without even a servant.

After a few days I began to find that whenever I played upon the vina at night, sitting on my bed, the bed would gradually begin to move as if levitating, and to rock to and fro. It would seem to rise for an instant some way into the air, but the movement was so smooth that there was no shock. I was playing with my eyes closed, and I thought that perhaps this was the effect of imagination under the spell of music.

This went on for some time. Then I happened to send my vina to be repaired, and one night to my great horror I heard a noise as if all the windows of my house were being smashed. I got up and looked everywhere. The windowpanes were unbroken, and there was no reason to suppose that there might be anyone in the house who had caused the noise. For three days this went on, and I could not sleep. I had no peace at night until my vina came back. The spirits seemed to be so much interested in my music that they rejoiced in it and showed their appreciation by lifting me up; when the food of their soul was not given they rebelled.

You may ask by what power the bed was lifted. The answer is that the finer forces are much more powerful than the external forces. There is nothing that they cannot lift up or carry.

An Exceptional Dog

I once had an experience with a dog. Returning from the theatre in the middle of the night with a few friends, I saw a dog following us. He showed a special interest in us.

One of us, thinking it to be a street dog, struck it with his stick. The instant that the stick hit it, the dog disappeared, and at the same moment the stick broke into pieces. This happened in the presence of many people.

We then found that a dog, a pet of our family, very fond of us, had died six months before. It was the spirit of that dog, still attached to us, that was following.

This dog was an exceptional one, and a remarkable thing about it was that every Thursday, regularly, it would fast.

A Majdhub in Baroda

I knew a majdhub in Baroda who was walking in the street at night. The policeman who was watching the street said to him, ''Who are you? Are you a thief?''

The majdhub said, ''Yes, I am a thief.''

The policeman took him to the police station, and there the majdhub spent the night, enjoying his experiences.

In the morning the officer came and said to the policeman, ''This is a majdhub whom you have arrested, not a thief.'' The policeman said, ''He said himself that he is a thief.'' When the officer spoke with him, he recognized him as a majdhub and he set him free.

When he was asked, ''Are you a thief?'', he said yes because whatever name or form comes before the consciousness of one who is lost in the Whole Being, he realizes as his self.

Interest and Indifference

I was very much amused once when visiting a certain town in India. I went into a shop to buy something, and the owner was sitting cross-legged on some cushions, smoking his pipe. I asked him whether he had the thing I wanted.

He thought for a moment or two and said, "I don't think so."

I asked, "Where can one get such a thing?"

He said, "I don't know."

He would not budge. He remained sitting quite comfortably where he was. I saluted him and thanked him for his kind silence and indifference.

Indifference is all right when one sits in meditation in the forest; but if one has a shop, what is needed is interest.

A Little Lower

In my early days of work I once came in contact with a family who were supposed to know music very well. When I went there they said, "We cannot have anything which is not up to the mark." I said, "That is what I want." "We have heard that you can give us some singing," they said. I said, "Yes," and then sang.

They said, "This is not what we want, excuse us." Well, I thought that I must sing something a little higher. So I sang again.

"This is not quite the thing we want either," they said. Then I understood what they wanted. So I sang something a little lower. They said, "This is somewhere nearer."

"Now," I thought, "I know what you want," and I sang something lower still. They said, "That is the best thing; that is what we wanted!"

Constancy

Once in India a man out hunting killed a bird, and saw as it fell to the ground that its mate flew down seeking after it. When he came near to take his prey he found the mate dead beside it. So impressed was he by the sight of the lifeless body lying beside its slaughtered mate that he never again went shooting.

Constancy never fails to impress by its beauty.

The Secret

There was in India a man called Rama Muti. He could lift elephants and stop motorcars running at full speed.

When this man, who was not extraordinary in build, was asked where he got this gigantic strength—for he looked like an ordinary human being, not like a monster—he said, "You know, and yet you do not know. The secret lies in the breath, which is all power."

Politeness

Once in India I was staying near a Hindu temple, and there were two porters who took care of that temple. They were Afghans, proud and rough, and rigid in their behavior; yet in their expression there was honesty and goodness.

Often I passed that way, and every time they ignored my entering and leaving, lest they should have the trouble of observing the conventional politeness.

One day one of them came to me with a message from his master. I got up from my seat and received him most cordially. And from that day, every time I passed I was well received, with smiles and a very cordial welcome, and they ignored me no more.

This happened because education was given to him without hurting his feelings; and as that gave him pleasure, he thought he would return the politeness.

A Sentence

I remember hearing for the first time in my life a sentence which made such a living impression upon me that I could not forget it for weeks together. Every time I pondered upon that sentence it brought a new light. And when I heard the sentence, it seemed as if it were spoken by my own soul, that my soul knew it, that it was never new but most dear and near to me.

It was a verse, a couplet; an address of a bubble to the sea. It runs:

Though I am a bubble and Thou art the sea,
Still I and Thou are not different.

It is a single sentence, but it went into my heart just like a seed thrown into fertile ground. From that time it continued to grow, and every time I thought about it, it brought me a new reflection.

A Telegraph Clerk

In a station in Rajputana I once saw a telegraph clerk accepting telegrams. While he was doing his work he was meditating at the same time.

When it was my turn I said to him, "I have come to give you this telegram, but I marvel at you. It is wonderful how you are keeping up your meditation during your work."

He looked at me and smiled; and we became friends.

The Turban

I had a friend in India who became cross very easily. Sometimes when he visited me I would say, "Are you cross today?"

He would ask, "Now how do you know I am cross today?"

I said, "Your turban tells me. The way you tie your turban wrongly shows disharmony."

Indifference as Love

Love can take many forms, even that of indifference.

I remember I went once, for a relative, to the house of a physician, an Indian physician who had a very ancient method of writing his prescriptions. Each took him nearly ten minutes. I was shown into a small room where fifteen to twenty people were already waiting, and I sat down among them. He continued to write prescriptions for all who came; and when he had finished with those who were before me, he began to write prescriptions for those who had come after me.

I had thought that the physician, as a friend of the family, would have seen me first, but he went on until he had seen everyone, and I was the last. Finally he said to me, "Now tell me what you want."

I told him, and he wrote out the prescription without any haste. When I was leaving he said, "I hope you understand that I did not want to see you while all the other patients were still there. I wanted to see you at leisure."

He was doing me a favor, and though he tried my patience, it was still a majestic sort of favor. It gave me a good example of love in the form of indifference.

Music Therapy?

Once the maharajah of Baroda, on hearing that healing could be accomplished through music, introduced concerts in certain hospitals.

The amusing result was that all those who were suffering began to cry out, "For God's sake, keep quiet! Go away!"

That was not the music to soothe them. It only made them suffer more; it was like giving a stone for bread.

In the Smoke

In Hyderabad there was a dervish who had the habit of smoking very strong hashish. When he let the smoke out of his mouth he used to look into it and answer any questions that were put to him. If someone asked him, "Where is my uncle at present?" he would say, "Your uncle? In Calcutta, near the bazaar, the second house on the left. Your uncle is sitting in his room, his servant is at his side, and his child is standing in front of him."

Whatever question he was asked, he answered. His consciousness had not the external self before it, and therefore it was able to see through the eyes of another, through the eyes of the uncle or any other. He did not see without eyes.

Muhammad Chehl

In twelve years' travelling throughout India, during which I concerned myself with psychical research, I met with great and extremely expert spiritualists, who were able to receive news in a moment from any part of the world and could even foretell future events by the help of a seer spirit.

Muhammad Chehl, a simple, unassuming man of ordinary appearance, our greatest spiritualist in India, showed the most wonderful phenomena. He could disconnect railway carriages from a train, leaving as many as he chose with the engine. Sometimes he disconnected all the carriages when the train was starting, leaving the engine to start alone.

He never cared to travel in any class but the third. He used often for fun to ask the people sitting in the same railway carriage to show him their tickets, and then he would take the tickets, tear them up, and throw them out of the window in their presence. Everybody was angry and wanted to fight with him.

He said to them, "Who has taken your tickets? You have them with you." He said to one, "Look in your turban"; to another, "Look again in your pocket"; to another, "See in your shoe"; to another, "Find it in your sleeve." They were all amused and thought him a wonderful conjurer.

He said to them, "You may think that I hid your tickets and then put them in your pockets by sleight of hand, but what do you think of this?" And he put his hand out of the window and asked for a few hundred tickets for Delhi, and a few hundred for Ajmer, and a few hundred for Agra, and he asked them what other stations they wanted.

When the train reached the next station there was great excitement. The stationmaster had just received a telegram saying that all the tickets for those stations had been stolen in a second and nobody knew where they had gone.

Muhammad Chehl never produced such phenomena unless he wanted to amuse himself. He never cared for notoriety or money. Nothing would induce him to make a show or a trade of his power. If he had cared to show his great power in the western world, he could have filled his house with bags of gold.

Mastery

I remember my teacher at school telling us that the leaves of the nim tree had great healing qualities. That did not interest me very much, but what did interest me was that, as he told us also, these leaves were so bitter that one could not drink a brew of them.

And the first thing I did was to gather some of the leaves. Nobody understood why I did it, but I made a tea of them and drank it, and to my great satisfaction I did not even make a face! For four or five days I continued this and then I forget all about it.

It is fighting against all that one cannot do that gives one mastery. But generally one does not do that; one fights against things that prevent one from getting what one wants. Man should fight only with himself, against the tendency of rejecting; this would lead him to mastery.

As a general principle in life there is no use in forcing anything. But if we want to train ourselves, that is another thing. It is a process, not a principle.

A Little Food

I came to Hyderabad, a young musician without any letter of recommendation, without any help to go to the nizam of Hyderabad. And I had great difficulty, such difficulty that I could not even speak about it to anyone. They thought, "What a presumption for a young man who has not yet made his name and built his reputation to even imagine such a thing!" Then I gave up seeing people and asking them for help. But the motive was there.

And then I happened to come in a place where a woman lived under the shade of a tree. They say she was in age more than a hundred years; some said she was three hundred years old, but I do not know. And she never spoke with people; she just sat there. A friend brought me to see this woman, and I at once felt that there was something wonderful about her. At that time she had an earthen bowl in her hand, and she was eating from it. As I went near to greet her, in answer to my greeting she took a little food in the same hand she was eating with and gave it to me. She had no fork. As she held it before me I first looked here and there, but my friend said, "Take it," so I at once stretched out my hand and took what she gave.

And the same week I was called to the court. I was presented at the court and had what I desired.

Memory

One day, six months after I had been received by my murshid as his pupil, he began to speak on metaphysics. Being metaphysically inclined myself, I eagerly welcomed the opportunity.

During those six months I was never impatient, I had never shown any eagerness to know more than what I was allowed to know. I was quite contented at the feet of the master; that was everything to me. Nevertheless it was a great stimulus to my mind to hear from him something about metaphysics. But as soon as I took out my notebook from my pocket my murshid ended the subject.

He said nothing; but from that day I learnt a lesson: "By this he means that my notebook must not be the storehouse of my knowledge. There is a living notebook; and that is my memory, a notebook which I shall carry with me all through life and through the hereafter."

Spiritual Education

In my youth my interest in the spiritual path was great, and I came in contact with the teacher by whom I was destined to be initiated. And the one thing my teacher said was, "No matter how great a teacher comes, once you have received this initiation, this blessing from my hands, your faith may not change."

Having had a modern education, I wondered what to think about this. I did not doubt, but I asked myself, "What does it mean?"

But with every step further in my life I found out more surely that this alone is the right way.

When the mind is disturbed, when a person is distrustful and goes first to one teacher and then tries another method, what can one find in him? There is no ideal there.

In a university one may study first under one professor and then under another, and so on. That is all right for a university; it is a different kind of education. But when it comes to spiritual education, idealism is necessary.

Acknowledging

Before I started looking for my teacher, the faculty of seeing was being developed in me. It is this which awakens the desire to seek for a teacher, for the teacher can give the explanation of life.

I did not tell my teacher about this faculty, for I was too impressed, too respectful, to speak of what I could see and hear. But one day, after having been with my teacher for some time, I ventured to speak about it.

And what was his answer? "I am sorry."

I was expecting a word of encouragement! But he added, "It is not seeing or hearing, it is acknowledging it that hinders one's progress."

Faith

I remember the blessing my spiritual teacher, my murshid, used to give me every time I parted from him. And that blessing was, "May your iman be strengthened."

At that time I had not thought about the word **iman.** On the contrary I thought as a young man, "Is my faith so weak that my teacher requires it to be stronger?" I would have preferred it if he had said, "May you become illuminated," or, "May your powers be great," or, "May your influence spread," or, "May you rise higher and higher," or, "May you become perfect." But this simple thing, "May your faith be strengthened," what did it mean?

I did not criticize, but I pondered and pondered upon the subject. And in the end I came to realize that no blessing is more valuable and important that this. For every blessing is attached to a conviction. Where there is no conviction there is nothing.

The secret of healing, the mystery of evolving, the power of all attainments, the way to spiritual realization all come from the strengthening of that belief which is a conviction, so that nothing can ever change it.

Perfect Relief

My murshid, Abu Hashim Madani, once said that there is only one virtue and one sin for a soul on the Sufi path: virtue when he is conscious of God, and sin when he is not.

No explanation can fully describe the truth of this except the experience of the contemplative. When he is conscious of God it is as if a window facing heaven were open, and when he is conscious of the self the experience is the opposite.

For all the tragedy of life is caused by being conscious of the self. All pain and depression are caused by this. Anything that can take away the thought of the self helps to a certain extent to relieve man from pain; but God-consciousness gives perfect relief.

Whom do You Torture?

I remember that when beginning to get interested in spiritual matters I once asked my teacher, "Murshid, do you approve of my staying up most of the night for my vigils?"

"Whom do you torture?" said my murshid. "Yourself? Is God pleased with it?"

I had not another word to say.

My Murshid's Servant

One day my murshid sent a man, a servant, with a message to me. I was coming in my usual way. And this servant, when he looked at me from a distance, thought, "This man must be so proud that he will not even look at me." The way I was dressed, the independent way I was walking, the way I was coming, that all showed him, "This man is so proud that he will not listen to me." He was poor, a servant, a porter; and so perhaps he saw the manifestation of it.

As soon as I came home, I asked, "What is it? Who are you? Where do you come from?" He said, "I have come from Madani Sahib."

As soon as I heard this, I took his hands, pressed them to my eyes, wanted to kiss his feet. The man was bewildered; he could not understand.

The Vision of My Murshid

I have had many experiences of the vision of my murshid, one of which is the following.

Once we were making a three days' journey through the jungle, in a place where there was great danger from robbers, and every night two or three travellers were killed.

Ours was the smallest caravan. Generally the caravans were of twenty wagons, but it happened that ours was of three wagons only. I had with me very precious gems given to me by the nizam of Hyderabad, and instead of arms I had musical instruments.

All night I saw the form of my murshid, at first faintly, afterwards distinctly, walking with the wagon. The two other wagons were attacked and robbed, and a few worthless bundles were taken, but my wagon was safe.

Gold-Embroidered Slippers

Once I looked at my murshid and there came to my inquisitive mind a thought, "Why should a great soul such as my murshid wear gold-embroidered slippers?"

But I checked myself at once, and it was only a thought. It could never have escaped my lips; it was under control. But there it was known. I could not cover my insolence with my lips; my heart was open before my murshid as an open book.

He instantly saw into it and read my thought. And do you know what answer he gave me? He said, "The treasure of the earth I have at my feet."

Rhythm

Once a murshid had been to the city, and on his return he said, "Oh, I am filled with joy, I am filled with joy. There was such an exaltation in the presence of the Beloved."

Then his mureed thought, "There was a beloved and an exaltation; how wonderful! I must go and see if I too cannot find one."

He went through the city, and when he came back he said, "Horrible! How terrible the world is! All seem to be at one another's throats; that was the picture I saw. I felt nothing but a depression, as if my whole being was torn to pieces." "Yes," the murshid said, "you are right."

"But explain to me," the mureed said, "why you are so exalted after going out, and why I must be so torn to pieces. I cannot bear it, it is horrible."

The murshid said, "You did not walk in the rhythm that I walked through the city."

Bijili

In the northern provinces near Nainital and Nepal, at the foot of the Himalayas, there is a jungle in which there are elephants. The natives have many different ways of catching these elephants, and one way is to dig a pit and cover it over with a net and branches; then they hang their hammocks up in the trees, and there they stay for some days watching for the elephants. They are quite happy in the trees because the climate is pleasant. If a herd of elephants happens to go that way, one elephant puts his foot in the net and falls into the pit; he cannot help himself. When he cries out, the other elephants look on from a distance but are afraid to go near; and the men have a kind of firework with which they frighten them away if they do.

Now in a troop of elephants there is always one which walks in front. He holds a stout branch in his trunk, and he knocks on the ground with it before every step to see whether there is a pit. Then, if the ground is safe, he goes forward and all the others follow him. He knows about a thousand other dangers. The herd have such confidence in him that wherever he goes,

they go too. This shows that the quality of leadership exists among elephants, and also the tendency to self-sacrifice. The elephant that is the leader goes first, realizing that if there is a pit he may fall in and the other elephants will be safe. He is careful, however, not to go anywhere where it is not safe, and if an elephant is caught it is generally some small elephant which has no sense and does not follow the leader.

In Nepal, the maharajah had an elephant which was just such a leader. He lived in the maharajah's palace, and the maharajah gave orders that no one should ride him but himself, because he honored the elephant, recognizing his qualities. I have seen this myself. Whenever Maharajah Bir Shamsher went into the forest elephant hunting, this elephant was taken too. The maharajah had named him Bijili, which means "lightning." He was very small, but if they failed to make a catch Bijili was sent out, and he always came back with another elephant.

He did not like to catch elephants; because he possessed the quality of mercy, he would never go unless he was forced by the mahouts. When he saw the other elephants at first he turned his head away. This shows that even among animals the prophetic tendency exists.

The Ideal Life

Once I was with a sage whom many people went to see. He pleased them all, and he was not fond of disputing or discussing, because to a sage there is nothing to discuss. Discussion is for those who say, "What I say is right, and what you say is wrong." A sage never says such a thing; hence there is no discussion. But the world is always fighting and discussing and disputing.

Many would come and try to dispute with him, but he did his best to avoid dispute. I was very fond of listening to his way of dealing with enquirers.

My friends wanted to discuss what the ideal life is. He said, "Whatever you think it is."

But my friends were not satisfied with this; they wanted a discussion. They answered, "Do you think this worldly life, with so many responsibilities, with strife from morning to evening, can be the ideal life?"

He said, "Yes."

They asked, "Do you not think that the life you lead, retirement and seclusion, is the ideal life?"

He answered, "Yes."

They said, "But how can we give up our present life, our responsibilities to our children, our occupations, and all these things that take up so much time? How can we leave that life in order to follow your ideal life?"

He said, "Do not leave it."

They went on, "But if we do not leave it, how can we get on in the spiritual life?"

Then the sage asked, "What do you mean by the spiritual life?"

"We mean by spiritual life a life like yours," they answered.

He said, "If you think my life is a spiritual life, be like me; if you think your life is a spiritual life, keep to it. It is not possible to say which life is best. If you think your worldly strife brings you happiness, just keep to it; if you think my life gives you happiness, give up your own. Whatever makes you happy and makes you think you are doing right, do it from that moment, and see what the result is. If it gives you more happiness, go on regardless of what others say. If it gives you happiness, if you are satisfied while doing it, while reaping its effect, then it is all right. Go on with it, and you will always be blessed."

His Life's Purpose

In these days there is the great drawback, that when people become very intelligent they lose their idealism. If they want to find God they want to find Him in figures. There are many who would rather meditate than worship, than pray. In this way there has always been conflict between the intellectual person and the idealistic person.

The Prophet was taught that the first thing is to idealize the Lord; and when the ideal he thus made became his conception of God, then in that conception God awakened. And he began to hear a voice saying, "Now you must serve your people; you must awaken in your people the sense of religion, the ideal of God, the desire for spiritual attainment, and the wish to live a better life."

Then he knew that it was now his turn to accomplish all those things that the prophets who had come before him had been meant to accomplish.

Everywhere

One day a man who had travelled very much saw an Indian mystic, and he said, "We have heard so much and read so much about the saints and sages and mahatmas and masters who live in India, but when I went there I found none."

And the mystic told him, "You need not have gone so far. The souls who are worthwhile, the souls who love one another, the saints and sages, are to be found everywhere."

A Thought of God

I was once in the presence of a very great saint and mystic. He was a classmate of my murshid. He performed many miracles and was much revered for his great love of humanity, and he advised everybody.

Someone came and said to him, "Please tell me the way to concentrate my mind. When I am in meditation a thousand thoughts come."

He said, "What thoughts, my brother?"

The man said, "I have so many things to do. There is my house, my business, my office. All these thoughts come when I wish to think of God."

The mystic said, "Every thought that comes, picture it as a thought of God. You cannot give an hour to God, as if that were a busines, and give the rest to your office."

Recognizing God

One day I was walking in the city and met a dervish with a beautiful personality. He was clothed in rags, but his speech, his voice, his thought, his movement, his atmosphere was so winning. At that time I was very young in the pursuit of philosophy. Youth is a time when pride has full play. So, as we were walking along and he called me "Murshid," I was very glad. He addressed me as murshid every time he spoke to me!

Presently we met another person who seemed to be without any education, without any knowledge of philosophy or religion or anything out of the way. But he called him "Murshid" also! My pride was broken, for next he came across a policeman and called him "Murshid" too!

I asked my teacher what could be the meaning of all this, and he said, "Your dervish shows you the first step towards recognizing God: to recognize all beings as your teacher. A foolish person can teach you, a wise person, a learned person, a student, a pious person, a wicked person, even a little child—everyone can teach you something. Therefore have that attitude towards everybody. Then it may be said that you recognize God."

The Emperors

When walking in a district where dervishes lived in solitude, I found ten or twelve dervishes together, sitting under the shade of a tree in their ragged clothes, talking to one another. As I was curious to hear and see people of different thoughts and ideas, I stood there watching this assembly to see what was going on.

These dervishes, sitting on the ground without a carpet, at first gave an impression of poverty and helplessness, sitting there in disappointment, probably entirely without possessions. But as they began to speak to each other that impression did not remain, for when they addressed one another they said, "O King of kings; O Emperor of emperors."

At first I was taken aback on hearing these words, but after giving some thought to it I asked myself, "What is an emperor, what is a king? Is the real king and emperor within or without?" For he who is the emperor of the outer empire depends on all that is without. The moment he is separated from that environment he is no longer an emperor. But these

dervishes sitting on the bare ground were real emperors. No one could take away their empire, for their empire, their kingdom, was not an illusion; theirs was a real kingdom. An emperor may have a bottle of wine in front of him, but these men had drunk that wine and had become real emperors.

The Tomb of Miran Datar

Many people who are obsessed go to Ujjain in central India to be healed at the tomb of a Sufi, Miran Datar, a saint who in his lifetime cured cases of obsession, and continued doing so even after death.

I once visited this place. On the steps of the tomb a man was sitting who seemed a quiet and thoughtful person. He was praying. If I had known that he was obsessed, I would not have spoken to him, but I did not know it, so I asked him, "Why are you here?"

He said, "Do not ask me such a question."

I said, "Why not?"

He said, "Because I am afraid. Now that I am near this holy tomb I have a little strength to answer you; if I were not here I could not even do that."

He told me that he had been a storekeeper on some British liner going back and forth between Bombay and London. One day at sea he had a strange feeling, as if some power were taking hold of him, and he was not able to do anything. After that this power would often take hold of him, and he could not do what he wanted to do. At times he wanted to eat but could not; at other times, when he did not want to eat, he had to go and eat. He became quite weak. He told the ship's doctor, but the doctor could do nothing for him. Then he went to see many other doctors, but none of them could help him. At last he went to the tomb of Miran Datar to see if he could find some relief.

While I was at the tomb of Miran Datar, the prince of Kerala came to it, a very handsome boy of twelve or thirteen accompanied by aides-de-camp and attendants. He was brought there to be cured. A conversation began of which we could hear only the part spoken by the prince, whose words were really those of the spirit that obsessed him. He said, "I will not leave him. I like him so much. He was in the forest, shooting, and he came near the tree on which I was sitting. Don't whip me, Miran, I am his guardian. I will not leave him. Miran, don't whip me."

The prince began to run, leaping high into the air, and showed every sign of being severely whipped. He ran round and round the tomb, leaping every time that the invisible whip struck the spirit. At last he fell down exhausted, and his attendants at once lifted him up and carried him away.

The Sage's Laughter

I once saw in India a sage whom I knew to be very deep, a man of high attainment, and he was laughing at nothing.

I wondered what he was laughing at. Then I stood there and looked around, thinking I must see from his point of view what was making him laugh so much. And I saw people hustling and bustling. For what? Was it not laughable? Every person thinking his particular point of view to be the most important!

Is this not the picture of life? Each person pushes others away because he finds his action the most important. It is the way of the evolved and the unevolved. And what do they reach? Nothing. Empty-handed they leave this world; they have come without anything and they leave without anything.

It is this outlook which bewilders the soul. The sage does not feel proud when he laughs at others, but at the same time he finds it highly amusing. And he is just as amused at himself as at others.

Seeing

Once I met a learned man, a doctor of philosophy with a great many degrees. We spoke about the deeper side of life. And he became very interested in what I said and told me that he thought very highly of me. So I thought how much more interesting it would be for him if I were to tell him about my teacher.

I told him, "There is a wonderful man in this city; he has no comparison in the whole world."

"Are there such people?" he asked. "I would very much like to see him. Where does he live?" And I told him, in such and such a part of the city.

He said, "I live there also. Where is his house? I know all the people there. What is his name?"

So I told him. He said, "For twenty years I have known this man, and now you are telling me about him!"

I thought to myself, "In a hundred years you would not have been able to know him."

He was not ready to know him. If people are not evolved enough they cannot appreciate, they cannot understand others. They cannot even understand the greatest souls. They may sit with them, talk with them; they may be in contact with them all their life, but they do not see. While another, if he is ready to understand, needs only one moment.

This philosopher had known my teacher for twenty years, and yet he did not know him. I saw him once and became his pupil forever. This man was learned, he was very intellectual, but he saw him with his brain: I saw my teacher with my heart.

A Bad Night

Once, on a journey, I had taken a room at Kandy in Ceylon. During the hours of my meditation in the evening, whilst I was engaged in the sacred practices, I felt very restless and disturbed, and could not fix my mind on my meditation for a single moment. I became cross with myself and went to bed, but my uneasiness increased.

Then I got up and felt I must look in the cupboards. I did not know why I was doing so. I think perhaps my inner self wanted to guide me to the reason for such an unusual experience. I found there, to my surprise, a bunch of black hair, looking as if some woman had collected her combings for a long time.

I spent a bad night, and in the morning the first thing I did was to ask the landlady who had occupied this room before me. She said, "Sir, don't remind me of her. The thought of her makes me feel ill. A woman lived here for some time. She never paid me my rent. She called me bad names, fought with the men, and quarrelled every single day, driving away all my tenants. Now my heart is at rest since she has left this house.''

I said, ''What a shame that you gave me such a room to stay in.''

She said, ''Sir, I gave you that room on purpose, because you seem from your looks to be a godly man, so that I was sure that this room would be purified by your good influence.''

I had no answer for her but a smile.

A Judge in Hyderabad

I myself knew in Hyderabad a judge, who was sitting all day in the law courts. At luncheon he heard a boy singing in the street. (In India the boys are very fond of singing in the street.) The boy was singing a very vulgar song.

The judge sent for the boy and made him sing the song. He made him sing it a second time, and then a third time, and again and again, a great many times.

The song was a very common song. The words were not made by a poet, and the music was not made by a musician. It was a lover singing to a girl, "You look at me as if you would eat me up," a very vulgar expression.

The judge saw all day how in the world each one tries to devour the other, to get the best of him; and the song moved him so much that from that day he took to a life of retirement. He gave everything away and became a dervish.

The Appointed Time

Once I put to music a verse of an inspired poet of Persia, and I sang it with great joy, for the words had a beautiful meaning. Yet at the same time I always felt that the verse had a meaning beyond the apparent one which I did not understand. I had a distinct feeling that something was sealed and hidden there.

And after fifteen years it happened, when my mind was searching for a simile for a certain revelation, that a voice came, bringing it to my mind. There was no end to my joy in opening that seal which had been closed for fifteen years!

For everything there is an appointed time; and when that time comes it is revealed. That is why, although on one hand we may be eager to attain to a certain revelation, yet on the other hand we must have patience to wait for the moment of its coming.

Mass Belief

Just before the war I was visiting Russia. In every shop one saw a picture of the czar and czarina, held in high esteem. It was a sacred thing for people. There was a religious ideal attached to the emperor, as he was the head of the church. And people used to be filled with joy when they saw the czar and czarina passing in the street; it was a religious upliftment for them.

But not long afterwards they had processions in the streets when at each step they broke the czarist emblems. It did not take them one moment to change their belief.

Why? Because it was a mass belief.

Living Teaching

A pupil I once had, who was very interested in spiritual exercises and metaphysical questions, left me and became a businessman. All his time was taken up with business, and he forgot me altogether. For ten years he never did his practices.

One day I happened to come to the city where he lived, and he remembered his old teacher who had returned. When he heard the lecture I gave, everything which he had been taught ten years before became alive in a moment; it was only too eager to come.

He said, "It is all living for me. Please tell me what to do." He was so eager to do things now.

And so it is. All that is in the mind, all one has never thought about, all that one never troubles about, is there; and when one has leisure from worldly occupations, it all becomes living.

The Path to Success

A friend who was a salesman in a big firm of jewelers used to come to me to talk philosophy. I was very interested in something he once told me.

He said, "It is very strange. I have seen so often on arriving at a house where I thought they were able to pay more than the actual price of things that I was tempted to ask a much higher price than what I knew the value to be; but every time I gave in to this temptation, I did not succeed.

"And again I was encouraged to do the same when I saw my fellow salesmen selling a stone to someone who took a fancy to it for a price perhaps four times its value.

"Why did they succeed and why do I not succeed?"

I told him, "Your way is different, their way is different. They can succeed by dishonesty; you can succeed by honesty. If you take their path, you will not succeed."

Forgetting Oneself

I remember a vina player, a very wonderful musician, who used to play and study many hours a day. But whenever he had to play before an audience he became self-conscious. The first thought that came to him was himself; and when that happened all the impressions of the people there would fall upon him. Generally he would then take his vina, cover it up, and run away.

On the other hand I have heard Sarah Bernhardt simply recite the *Marseillaise*, that was all. But when she appeared on the stage and recited this poem, she would win every heart in the audience, for at that time—it was during the war—she was France. What enabled her to be France was her concentration, her way of forgetting herself.

Duty

At the time of the last war there was a young woman who was always displeased and in disagreement with her husband, and was always wanting a separation. When the call to arms came her husband went to the battlefield, and he hoped that in his absence she would find someone else.

As the war went on she thought that while her husband was fighting she would enroll as a nurse. And it happened that near the place where she was working her husband was wounded. He lost his eyes, and she became his nurse.

When she saw him in that condition she was astonished that it had so come about that she was to be his nurse. She had just received a letter containing a proposal of marriage, but she tore it up and changed her mind in an instant. She said, "Now that he has lost his eyes and is helpless, I shall remain his wife. I shall take care of him all his life."

Luther Burbank

Some say animals have no mind. But that is a wrong conception. Wherever there is a body there is a mind; even the tree has a mind.

Luther Burbank once said to me in support of this argument, "You should watch the tendency of a plant, what is its inclination. For if you do not watch it, the plant will not grow fully. I treat them as living beings. They speak to me, and I to them."

No Division

Sometimes the mystery of life is known to a person. He may not be a mystic, but if his time comes, he knows it.

One day I was interested when a man who had done nothing but business all his life and made himself so rich that he was perhaps one of the richest men in the country wanted to show me his park, a beautiful park he had around his house.

While I was his guest we were taking a walk. He said, "It is wonderful to come here into my park in the morning and evening."

I asked him, "How far does your park extend?"

And he said, "Do you want to know? Do you see the horizon from here?"

I said, "Yes."

He told me, "All this land is mine and the sea besides. All that you can see."

It was a wonderful answer: he was not only conscious of what he possessed, but of all that was there. He did not make a dividing line between what was his own and what was beyond.

Mr. Ford

People say that a mystic is someone who dreams and who lives in the clouds. My answer to this is that the real mystic stands on earth, but his head is in heaven. It is not true that the wise man is not intellectual or that the wise man is not clever. A clever man is not necessarily wise, but the one who has the higher knowledge has no difficulty in gaining knowledge of worldly things. It is the man who has knowledge of worldly things only who has great difficulty in absorbing the higher knowledge.

Mr. Ford was very wise when he said to me, "If you had been a businessman, I am sure you would have been successful."

Furthermore, he said, "I have tried all my life to solve the problem which you appear to have solved."

This again gives us an insight into the idea that higher wisdom does not debar a person from having worldly wisdom, though worldly wisdom does not qualify a person to attain to the higher wisdom.

A Warning

An artist related how his father, whom he greatly respected, gave him no rules of conduct, but treated him always with trust and confidence; and how it was from his brother-in-law, the husband of his older sister, that he received as a child a much needed warning.

The brother-in-law, seeing the ardor, the generosity, the sociability, the enthusiasm for life of the youth, took him to various parts of the town, pointing out the different types of humanity; reminding him at the same time of the great traditions of his race and of his family, of the ideals of his fathers, of the beauty and pride of nobility.

What he pointed out and what the youth saw with his own eyes left an undying impression on his mind of the effects of perversion, influencing the whole trend of his life.

Youth is generous, youth is ardent, and youth rarely fails to respond.

The Childish Attitude

Once I was introduced in New York to a scientist who was also a philosopher. The first thing he said about his accomplishments was, "I have discovered the soul."

It amused me very much that while all the scriptures, thinkers, mystics, and prophets have spoken about it, this man should come and say, "I have discovered the soul!"

I thought, "Yes, that was the new discovery that we were expecting, something that we never knew."

Such is the attitude of mind today, the childish attitude.

When one looks into the past, the present, and the future, one sees that life is eternal; and what one can discover is that which has always been discovered by those who seek.

Suddenly

There was a girl who had learned a new theatrical song, the words of which were, "How suddenly my fate has changed!" She took such a liking to it that wherever she was about the house, she hummed it and she said the words.

And what was the outcome? She was looking down from a balcony of the house, and she fell from it and was killed. Those who knew her said she was particularly happy three days before she began singing this song.

Imagination

Once I visited a school of thought culture. They had made a new system, and I went to see it.

There were ten or twelve children standing there, and the teacher said, "Look, what is there here?" There was nothing but a plain board before them. One child said, "A lily." The teacher said, "All right." To another child he said, "Look, what is here?" The other child looked and said, "A red rose." The teacher was satisfied. And to the third child he said, "See, what is here?" The child said, "It is a pink rose," and again the teacher was satisfied.

Then he asked another child to tell what was there, and the child said, "I do not see anything." I thought to myself, "He is the one who has some sense, for he did not tell a lie."

Silence

I was very much interested in what Mme. Montessori told me when I was in Italy: that besides all the activities that she gives to children, she makes them keep silence; and after a little time they like it so much that they prefer silence to their activity.

And it interested me still more to see a little girl of about six years of age who, when the time of silence came, went and closed the windows and closed the door, and put away all the things that she was playing with. Then she came and sat in her little chair and closed her eyes, and she did not open them for about three or four minutes. You could see on her innocent face an angelic expression. It seemed she preferred those five minutes of silence to all the playing of the whole day.

A Child's Question

Once a nurse came to me with a child and said, "This child asks wonderful questions, and I cannot answer them."

I said, "What are the questions?"

She replied, "When the child was going to say its evening prayer before going to bed, it asked me, 'If God is in heaven, up in heaven, then why must I bow low to the earth?'"

The nurse was very perplexed; she did not know how to answer. But if the child had not been answered, from that moment its belief would have gone, because that is the time when the soul is beginning to enquire into life and its mystery.

I asked the child, "What did you say?" The child explained it to me, and I said, "Yes, God is in heaven, but where are His feet? On the earth. By bending towards the earth, you are touching His feet."

It was quite satisfied.

Resist Not Evil

I was once asked how anyone at the head of a busines or institution could possibly keep to the rule of not resisting evil. I said that I had seen people at the heads of certain factories who had won the hearts of everyone working there, while there were other directors against whom every worker in the factory was speaking. It may be that the latter made a greater profit than the former, yet in the end they would find the gain of the former to be more enduring than their own.

The ways of wisdom and tenderness cannot be made into a restricted principle for people to follow. A brush can never take the place of a knife, and therefore we all have to use every method and activity according to the circumstances. Nevertheless, the thought of not resisting evil should always be in the background.

Not Acknowledging

Once a friend came to me and said, "I do not know what bad planet is exerting its influence upon me, but for the last three years everything I touch has gone wrong; nothing brings success or pleasure."

I said, "I am very sorry you have come so late, yet it is not too late. But for three years you have added fuel to this fire."

Then he asked, "How did I add fuel to this fire?"

I answered, "By acknowledging it."

If we acknowledge every little fact that has a bad effect upon our life, we give it life from our own, and thus make it a living thing.

And so it is with many illnesses. Very often people get into the habit of saying, "Oh, I am so tired!" It is not necessary for them to cut wood or carry stones, they will be tired before doing it. No sooner do they think of tiredness than it is there. There are many cases in which there is no need to be tired; one becomes tired only by the fact of having acknowledged it.

It is the same with sleeplessness. Once one acknowledges to oneself that one cannot sleep, that is enough to keep one awake all night.

There are many illnesses of this kind, and chief among them is depression.

The Doctor Died

I knew a person whom a physician had examined and had told that he would die in three months. No doubt if that person had been imaginative he would have taken that impression. But he came to me and he said, "What nonsense! Die in three months! I am not going to die even in three hundred years."

And to our great surprise within three months the doctor died, and this man brought me the news!

We must learn to respect the human being and realize that a human soul is beyond birth and death, that a human soul has a divine spirit in it, and that all illnesses and pains and sufferings are only his tests and trials. He is above them, and we must try to raise him above illness.

Neuritis

Once I met a lady who said she had been to many physicians for the complaint of neuritis. She was temporarily cured, but it always came back, and she asked me for something that would help her.

I said to her, "Is there any person in the world whom you dislike, whom you hate, or whose action is troubling your mind?"

She said, "Yes, there are many people whom I dislike, and especially there is one person whom I cannot forgive."

"Well," I said, "that is the neuritis, that is the root of the disease. Outwardly it is a pain of the body; inwardly it is rooted in the heart."

The Opera

The great pity in the world of sound today is that people are going far away from what is called the natural voice; and this is brought about by commercialism.

First a hall was made for one hundred persons, then for five hundred, and then for five thousand. A man must shout to make five thousand people hear him in order to have a success. And that success is one of the ticket office.

But the magical charm lies in the natural voice. Every person is gifted; God has given him a certain pitch, a natural note. If he develops that note it is magic; he can perform a miracle. But today he must think about the hall where he has to sing, and of how loud he must shout.

There was a man from India visiting Paris, and for the first time in his life he went to the opera to hear the music there. He tried hard to enjoy it. The first thing he heard was a soprano doing her best. Then came the tenor or baritone, and he had to sing with her.

That made this man very annoyed and he said, "Now look! He has come to spoil it!"

Red Walls

Once I was visiting a house which had been taken by a certain club. One of the members told me, "It is a very great pity; since we have taken this house, there is always disagreement in our committee."

I said, "No wonder. I see it."

They asked, "Why?"

I said, "The walls are red. They make you inclined to fight."

The Kaiser's Palace

Whether the artist knows it or not, what he makes always has an influence.

Once when I was visiting Berlin I saw some statuary round the kaiser's palace, and when I looked at it I thought that it was no wonder that this empire had collapsed. It could not have been otherwise: it was as if the statues had been put there on purpose in order to ruin it! The symbolism which, either consciously or unconsciously, the artist had embodied in these statues was nothing but a source of ruin.

Even now or at some future time, if anyone lives there, he will meet his downfall. It cannot be otherwise.

Inner Peace

Once I was with a man who was in the habit of meditating. While we were sitting near the fire and talking about things he went into the silence, and I had to sit quiet until he opened his eyes.

I asked him, "It is beautiful, is it not?" And he said, "It is never enough."

Those who experience the joy of meditation, for them there is nothing in this world which is more interesting and enjoyable. They experience the inner peace and the joy that cannot be explained in words. They touch perfection, or the spirit of light, of life, and of love—all is there.

A Little Indifference

There was a small group of people in London who were working along spiritual lines. They felt a sort of rivalry against my little society, and they began to try to do us harm by telling stories against us and by setting others against us. My helpers came to tell me how we were being damaged in this way and asked if they should not do something to stop it. But I answered, "The best way to treat this is with indifference. Take no notice."

And when they insisted that these doings would do us great harm I said, "Not at all. The only harm it could do would be if we allowed this harm to enter our circle. Let them do as they like and let us go on doing what we are doing!"

As the years went by they never heard us say a word against them; on the contrary, we welcomed them, we helped them, we served them in whatever way we could. In time this resistance completely vanished. We have been going forward, and they still stand where they were. Just a little indifference was enough!

The Man in the Street

One day I was introduced to a very well-known poet by a friend immediately after I had given a lecture. And this poet asked me, "Is it really true that inspiration is required for poetry?" He, a well-known poet, did not believe in inspiration!

And I met another poet who had made a great name for himself, but neither his expression nor his movements, words, or thoughts showed any sign of his being a poet. Why was this so? Because to become well-known and enjoy momentary success, a man nowadays has to come down to the lowest mentality; that is what makes him a great man in the eyes of people today.

But it is a mistake. Why must one impress common people? It is better to impress the best people, the people with the purest mentality and highest spirit, and let the others appreciate what is shallow. In this way one can raise the ordinary people to a higher standard instead of stooping to reach them on their own level.

In New York a newspaper reporter came to see me and

asked questions for half an hour, questions on philosophy and mysticism. I was so interested in the questions he asked that I answered them extensively. Finally the journalist said, "How shall I put all these things that you have told me to the man in the street?"

I said, "If you have come here in order to put these ideas to the man in the street, please do not use any of them; just put what you like."

And so he did.

The Horizon

Once when I was sailing in a boat, a sailor gave me some interesting advice. I asked him if he knew any remedy against seasickness, and he said, "No, they have tried for a long time to find something, but nothing is any good. You must fix your eyes on the horizon; that will keep you from being seasick."

I was greatly benefited by that advice, and it was a stimulus to my imagination, showing that the wider the outlook, the less are the troubles in life. If we fix our eyes on the horizon, as far as we can see, then we are saved from the little things which make our life unhappy.

God is the horizon, as far as our sight extends and even further, for we can neither touch the horizon nor can we touch God.

The Doors of Hearing

An adept was sitting in a ship with an ordinary person, and this person said, "Oh, how terrible this noise is, continually going on! It breaks my nerves to pieces. Terrible, terrible, terrible! To hear this going on day and night almost drives me mad!"

The adept said, "I did not hear it until you reminded me of it. I hear it when I want to hear it; I do not hear it when I do not want to hear it."

That is the idea. Both had the sense of hearing, but one had the power to close it and to open it. The other had the doors of his sense of hearing open but he could not close them.

Dig Deep

Someone came to me and said, "I was very sympathetic once, but somehow I have become hardened. What is the reason for it?"

I said, "You tried to get water from the bottom of the earth. But instead of digging deep down you dug in the mud, and you were disappointed. If you have patience to dig till you reach water then you will not be disappointed."

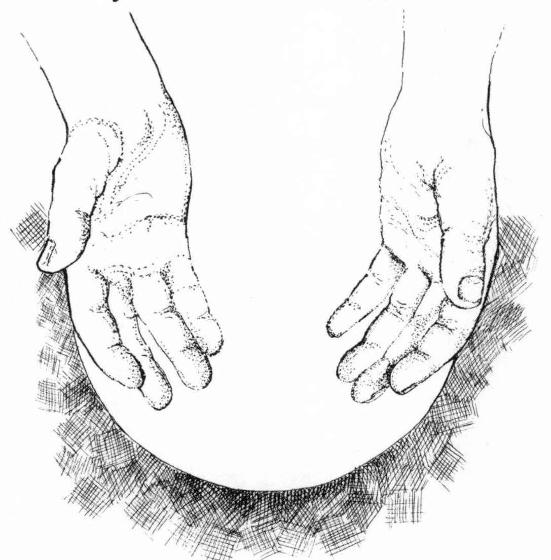

Your Servant, Sir

Once when travelling I met a man of a very dense evolution, a soldier who always lived in military surroundings and who had very fixed ideas of his own. And when we were talking together and it appeared that we thought differently about something, I happened to say in order to preserve harmony, "Well, we are brothers!"

He looked at me with great anger, and said, "Brothers! How dare you say such a thing!"

I said, "I forgot. I am your servant, Sir."

He was very pleased. I could have argued, but this would have created disharmony without reason. The foolishness of that man blazed up just like fire; I put water on it and extinguished it. I did not diminish myself, for we are all servants of one another; and it pleased and satisfied him.

Patience

A young man one day showed some impatience with his aged father, who could not hear very clearly anymore and asked him two or three times to repeat what he had said.

Seeing the irritated expression on his face, the father said, "My son, do you remember that there was a day when you were a little child and you asked me what a certain bird was and I told you a sparrow? You asked me perhaps fifty times, and I had the patience to repeat it to you again and again without being hurt or troubled about it; I was only pleased to tell you all I knew.

"Now when I can no longer hear so well, you can at least have patience with me and explain something twice if I did not hear you the first time."

A Faithful Friend

I remember going to see a patient who had been suffering from an illness for more than twenty years and had lost every hope of getting better. Several physicians had been consulted, and many different treatments had been tried.

I told her a simple thing to do; I did not teach any special practices, but just an ordinary little thing to do in the morning and in the evening. And to the great surprise of those at home, she began to move her hands and legs, which had been thought impossible. This gave them great hope, that a patient who had been so long in bed could do this, and to her too it was a great surprise.

I went to see them after a few days and asked them, "How is the patient progressing?"

They said, "She is progressing very well. We could never have believed that she could move her hands and legs; it is the most wonderful thing. But we cannot make her believe that now after twenty years of suffering she can ever be well again. This illness has made such an impression upon her that she thinks that it is natural for her, and that to be well is a dream, an unreality."

This gave me the idea that when a person lives in a certain condition for a long, long time, that condition becomes his friend unconsciously. He does not know it, he may think that he wants to get out of it, yet there is some part of his being that is holding his illness just the same.

One day, remembering this pecularity of human nature, I asked someone who was brought to me to be cured of an obsession how long she had had this obsession.

She explained to me how horrible the obsession was, how terrible life was for her.

I listened for half an hour to everything that she said against the obsession; but recollecting this amusing aspect of human nature, I asked her, "You do not really mean to say that you want to get rid of that spirit? If I had this spirit I would keep it. After all these years that you have had it, it seems unjust and very cruel to the spirit. If this spirit had not cared for you, it would not have stayed with you. In this world, is it easy for a person to remain so long with one? This spirit is most faithful."

Then she said, "I do not really want to get rid of it."

I was very much amused to see how this person wanted sympathy and help, but did not want to give up the spirit. It was not the spirit that was obsessing the person, but the person obsessing the spirit!

Impossible

Once I was at a reception at a friend's house, and there was someone there who disputed with every guest, so that they were all tired out.

I tried to avoid him, but someone introduced us; and when he heard that I was a teacher of philosophy, he thought, "This is the person I want." And the first thing he said was, "I do not believe in God."

I said, "Do you not? But do you believe in this manifestation and in the beauty of this world of variety, and that there is a power behind it which produces all this?"

He said, "I believe in all that, but why should I worship a personality, why should I call him God? I believe in it but I don't call it God."

I said to him, "You believe that every effect has a cause, and that for all these causes there must be an original cause. You call it cause, I call it God; it is the same. There is some officer whom you salute; some superior before whom you bow, for instance your father or mother; some fair one whom you love and adore, for whom you have a feeling of respect; some power before which you feel helpless. How great then must that person be who has produced and controls all this, and how much more worthy of worship!"

He answered, "But I do not call that a divinity, I call it a universal power, an affinity working mechanically, harmonizing all."

When I tried to keep him to one point, he ran to another; and when I followed him there, he ran to another; until at last I ceased, thinking of the words of Shankaracharya,

All impossible things can be made possible
Save the bringing of the fool's mind to the point of truth.

Eternal Matter

I once met a young man who said to me, "I do not believe in God, the hereafter, or the soul."

I told him that I did not wish to make him believe in these things, that this was not my intention at all. But then the young man asked me what I believed, for he wanted to continue our conversation.

I said, "It is very difficult to put one's belief into words, but I would very much like you to tell me first what you believe."

He said very easily, "I believe in eternal matter."

I said, "My belief is not very far from yours, for the very same thing that you call eternal matter, I call eternal spirit. It is a difference of words; we really believe the same thing."

Matter cannot be eternal, but if the young man wished to call that which is eternal matter, I had no objection; I was quite willing to call it matter too.

Mental Illness

Once I happened to go to an asylum for the insane in New York, and the physicians very kindly laid before me a number of skulls showing different cavities in the brain and spots of decay which had caused insanity in the lives of the patients. There is always a sign of it in the patient's physical body. It may be apparent suffering or it may be some decay at the back of it, yet it is not known.

I asked them, "I would like to know whether the cavity brought about the insanity or the insanity brought about the cavity?"

Their argument was that the cavity brought about the insanity. But mental disorder is not always caused by a cavity in the brain, for the inner being has a greater influence on the physical being than the physical body has on the mental existence. Yet it is not always the mind that brings about the physical illness; very often it is so, but not always.

A Wise Man

I was once talking to a businessman, a man who had spent nearly fifty years of his life in commerce and had made a success of it.

He had never believed in any religion, he had never studied any philosophy except that sometimes he read the works of great poets. But after we had talked for about an hour on subjects concerning the inner life, he discovered that he was not very far from my own beliefs; that after all, the patience which is required to make money, the sacrifices one has to make in order to be successful, and the experiences one has to go through with those whom one works with daily in business, had been for him both a practice and a study.

And I found that he was not very far from the conclusions to which a wise man, a philosopher, a mystic would come. It is he whom I would call a wise man, for by his wisdom he had reached the truth which is studied by the philosopher and which is attained by the mystic through meditation.

Freedom

On one occasion I was amused to hear a man say, "The condition of our country? We have so much freedom that we do not know what to do with it!"

It is the same with a person who can see and hear; he finds so much to see that he does not know what to do. The Sufi, therefore, is grateful for what he sees and hears, and also grateful for what he does not see and hear. He learns resignation on the path of the divine voyage.

Enough

Sometimes people come to me and say, "I have thought about something and I wanted it, but I never got it."

And I have answered, "You never wanted it. If you had wanted it you would have got it."

They do not believe this; they continue to think that they wanted it. It may be so, but to want it enough is another thing.

Paderewski

I once had the pleasure of hearing Paderewski in his own house.

He began to play gently on his piano. Every note took him into a deeper and deeper ocean of music. Any meditative person could see clearly that he was so concentrated in what he did that he knew not where he was.

The End of the World

One day a person put some colors on paper and showed it to me, saying, ''People cannot understand this deep idea, but you will understand it. It is very deep: it has come from some clairvoyant source.''

I looked at it. There were many colors, that was all one could say. They were not even blending harmoniously with one another, they were only striking.

The person who had painted it looked at me and waited for my opinion. He said, ''What do you think of it?''

So I said, ''It is a picture of the end of the world.''

And he was very pleased with this answer.

8492